CHAPTER 1:

The effective deployment of deception techniques in cybersecurity relies heavily on a well-considered strategy that aligns with an organization's overall security objectives. This approach demands not only a clear understanding of the individual components of deception—such as honeypots, decoys, and traps—but also an integration of these elements into a cohesive defense mechanism. Each technique must be tailored to fit the specific needs and vulnerabilities of the organization's environment, creating a multi-faceted security posture that maximizes both deterrence and detection.

In practice, implementing deception strategies involves a series of deliberate steps that begin with an assessment of the organization's threat landscape and existing security infrastructure. This initial phase is crucial, as it determines how deception can be best utilized to address specific security gaps. The deployment of honeypots, for instance, requires careful planning to ensure that they do not inadvertently create additional vulnerabilities. A well-designed honeypot must simulate realistic interactions that can attract potential attackers while remaining isolated from the core network to prevent any spillover effects.

Decoys, by contrast, are often integrated into the existing network environment and require a different approach. The effectiveness of decoys hinges on their ability to blend seamlessly with legitimate assets, thereby creating a convincing illusion of valuable resources. This involves strategically placing decoys in areas where they are likely to be encountered by attackers, such as high-traffic segments of the network or within critical systems. The success of decoys depends on their ability to provide false leads without drawing undue attention or disrupting legitimate operations.

Traps are another critical element of the deception toolkit, designed to capture and analyze specific types of malicious activities. Unlike honeypots and decoys, which focus on broader deception strategies, traps are engineered to trigger responses from attackers based on predefined actions. This requires a deep understanding of typical attacker behavior and the ability to create scenarios that will elicit a reaction. For instance, a trap might involve baiting an attacker with a fake vulnerability or a piece of sensitive information that, when accessed, activates logging mechanisms to capture detailed data about the attacker's tactics and tools.

The integration of these deception techniques into a broader security strategy also necessitates ongoing management and refinement. Deception systems must be continuously monitored to ensure they remain effective and relevant. This involves regularly updating honeypots and decoys to reflect changes in the threat landscape and adapting traps to address emerging attack patterns. Additionally, the data collected from deception techniques must be analyzed and used to inform broader security measures, such as updating threat intelligence feeds and adjusting defensive configurations.

A key aspect of managing deception strategies is ensuring that they do not create false positives or disrupt legitimate activities. For example, the presence of a honeypot or decoy must be carefully managed to avoid alerting genuine users or causing confusion within the network. Similarly, traps must be designed to capture relevant data without generating excessive noise or overwhelming security analysts with irrelevant information. Balancing these considerations requires a nuanced approach that combines technical expertise with a thorough understanding of the organization's operational environment.

Another important consideration in the deployment of deception techniques is the legal and ethical implications. While deception can be a powerful tool for enhancing security, it must be implemented in a manner that complies with legal and regulatory requirements. This includes ensuring that the use of honeypots, decoys, and traps does not violate privacy laws or other legal constraints. Additionally, organizations must be mindful of the potential ethical implications of using deceptive techniques, particularly in relation to the treatment of individuals who may inadvertently interact with deceptive systems.

The effectiveness of cybersecurity deception is also influenced by the broader context in which it is employed. This includes the organizational culture and the level of awareness among employees regarding cybersecurity practices. A culture that promotes vigilance and an understanding of deceptive tactics can enhance the overall effectiveness of these strategies. Conversely, a lack of awareness or training may undermine the benefits of deception by leading to misunderstandings or mishandling of deceptive systems.

In conclusion, the implementation of cybersecurity deception techniques requires a comprehensive approach that integrates these elements into a well-defined security strategy. This involves careful planning, continuous management, and ongoing refinement to ensure that deception techniques are effectively deployed and aligned with the organization's security objectives. By understanding the nuances of honeypots, decoys, and traps, and by addressing the legal, ethical, and operational considerations, organizations can leverage deception as a powerful tool in their overall security arsenal.

The successful integration of deception techniques into an organization's security strategy is not merely a matter of technical deployment but also involves a strategic alignment with broader security objectives and practices. To ensure the effectiveness of these techniques, it is essential to consider the interplay between deception and other security measures, as well as the continuous adaptation to evolving threats.

One of the critical aspects of leveraging deception effectively is its integration with traditional security controls. While deception techniques such as honeypots, decoys, and traps provide valuable insights and deterrents, they are not a panacea for all security challenges. Instead, they must complement and enhance existing security measures, including firewalls, intrusion detection systems, and access controls. For example, honeypots can be used in conjunction with intrusion detection systems to provide additional context and validation for alerts. By analyzing the data collected from honeypots, security teams can improve their ability to distinguish between genuine threats and false positives, thereby enhancing the overall effectiveness of their detection capabilities.

Furthermore, the deployment of deception techniques should be guided by a well-defined strategy that aligns with the organization's risk management framework. This involves identifying key assets and potential attack vectors, and designing deception tactics that address specific threats. For instance, if an organization is particularly concerned about data exfiltration, it might deploy traps designed to capture attempts to access sensitive information. Conversely, if the focus is on preventing unauthorized access to critical infrastructure, decoys might be placed in network segments where attackers are likely to probe for vulnerabilities. By tailoring deception strategies to address specific risk factors, organizations can optimize their security posture and make more efficient use of their resources.

Another important consideration is the role of deception in incident response and threat intelligence. The data gathered from deception techniques can provide invaluable insights into attacker behavior, techniques, and tools. This information can be used to inform incident response efforts by identifying the methods and objectives of attackers, which in turn helps to develop more effective countermeasures. Additionally, threat intelligence derived from deception can enhance an organization's understanding of emerging threats and trends, allowing for proactive adjustments to security measures and strategies.

To fully capitalize on the benefits of deception, organizations must also invest in training and awareness programs for their security personnel. Understanding how to interpret and act upon the information generated by deception techniques is crucial for maximizing their effectiveness. Security teams must be well-versed in the operational aspects of honeypots, decoys, and traps, and be able to integrate this information into their broader security operations. Regular training and exercises can help ensure that personnel are prepared to respond effectively to the insights provided by deception techniques and to adapt their strategies in response to evolving threats.

The effectiveness of deception also hinges on continuous evaluation and refinement. The threat landscape is dynamic, with new attack methods and techniques emerging regularly. To maintain the relevance and effectiveness of deception strategies, organizations must engage in ongoing assessment and adjustment of their deception tactics. This includes regularly reviewing and updating honeypots, decoys, and traps to ensure they reflect current attack trends and do not become outdated or ineffective. Additionally, organizations should evaluate the performance of their deception techniques through metrics and feedback mechanisms, allowing for data-driven improvements and optimizations.

Ethical and legal considerations remain a significant factor in the deployment of deception techniques. As organizations implement deceptive measures, they must remain vigilant to ensure compliance with relevant regulations and legal frameworks. This includes safeguarding personal data, respecting privacy rights, and ensuring that deceptive practices do not inadvertently harm legitimate users or systems. Developing clear policies and procedures for the use of deception, and involving legal and ethical advisors in the planning and implementation phases, can help mitigate potential risks and ensure that deception techniques are used responsibly and within legal boundaries.

Ultimately, the role of deception in cybersecurity is to provide an additional layer of defense by creating an environment where attackers are misled and their actions are exposed. This approach not only enhances the detection and understanding of threats but also contributes to a more resilient and adaptive security posture. By effectively integrating deception techniques with traditional security controls, aligning them with risk management practices, and continuously refining their implementation, organizations can leverage deception as a powerful tool in their overall security strategy.

In conclusion, the deployment of cybersecurity deception requires a comprehensive approach that integrates technical, strategic, and operational considerations. By understanding the intricacies of honeypots, decoys, and traps, and by addressing the associated challenges and considerations, organizations can harness the full potential of deception to enhance their security defenses. Through careful planning, continuous monitoring, and ongoing adaptation, deception techniques can provide a valuable asset in the fight against cyber threats, contributing to a more robust and effective security posture.

CHAPTER 2:

Understanding the psychological tactics that underpin successful cyber attacks is essential for both identifying vulnerabilities and crafting effective defense strategies. One of the most significant areas of psychological manipulation in cybersecurity is the exploitation of social influence techniques. These techniques rely on social and psychological factors to sway behavior, making them highly effective in deceptive practices.

Social proof is one such technique that attackers frequently exploit. This principle is based on the idea that individuals are more likely to comply with requests or follow actions that they perceive others as also following. In a cybersecurity context, attackers may use social proof by presenting information that suggests that a particular action or response is common or endorsed by many others. For example, a phishing email might falsely indicate that a security update is being implemented company-wide, encouraging targets to click on malicious links or provide sensitive information under the guise of following standard procedure.

Another powerful social influence technique is the principle of commitment and consistency. This principle suggests that once individuals commit to an action or stance, they are more likely to remain consistent with that commitment. Attackers leverage this by creating situations where targets make small, seemingly innocuous commitments, which then lead to larger, more consequential actions. For instance, an attacker might first ask a target to provide minimal information or complete a trivial task, gradually escalating to requests for more sensitive data. The initial commitment creates a psychological pressure to maintain consistency, making it more likely that the target will comply with subsequent, more significant demands.

The concept of reciprocity also plays a crucial role in the psychology of deception. In social interactions, reciprocity involves the mutual exchange of favors or concessions, and this principle is harnessed by attackers to manipulate targets. By offering something of perceived value or benefit, attackers can create a sense of obligation in their targets. This might manifest as offering a free trial or an enticing reward in exchange for personal information. The principle of reciprocity exploits the natural inclination to return favors, making targets more susceptible to providing sensitive data or performing actions that further the attacker's goals.

In addition to these social influence techniques, attackers frequently exploit the psychological principle of fear and urgency. By instilling a sense of panic or immediate threat, attackers can bypass normal decision-making processes and prompt rapid, often irrational, responses. For example, a common tactic is to send urgent alerts claiming that an account will be suspended or compromised unless immediate action is taken. The fear of losing access to critical services or data drives individuals to act hastily, often without thoroughly evaluating the legitimacy of the request. This manipulation of emotional responses is particularly effective in eliciting compliance and bypassing security protocols.

On the defensive side, understanding these psychological principles enables the development of strategies to counteract the influence of deceptive tactics. For example, security awareness training programs can be designed to educate users about the techniques attackers use, such as social proof, reciprocity, and urgency. By increasing awareness and providing practical guidance on how to recognize and resist these tactics, organizations can reduce the effectiveness of social engineering attacks. Training should include scenarios that highlight common psychological manipulations and provide strategies for verifying the authenticity of communications and requests.

Moreover, organizations can incorporate psychological principles into their own deception strategies to enhance security. For instance, creating decoy systems that exploit the principle of commitment and consistency can be effective in trapping attackers. By simulating a scenario where attackers are led to make small commitments, organizations can observe their behavior and gather valuable intelligence. Similarly, deploying traps that induce a sense of urgency or fear can help in capturing attackers' actions and understanding their methods.

The ethical considerations surrounding the use of psychological tactics in both offensive and defensive contexts are paramount. While exploiting psychological principles can enhance security, it is crucial to ensure that these tactics are used responsibly and do not infringe on privacy or ethical boundaries. For instance, when deploying deceptive elements, organizations must be careful to avoid causing unnecessary distress or violating legal standards. Establishing clear policies and ethical guidelines for the use of psychological tactics can help in maintaining a balance between effective security measures and ethical practices.

In conclusion, the psychology of deception plays a fundamental role in understanding and defending against cyber threats. By examining how social influence techniques, cognitive biases, and emotional responses are leveraged in cyber attacks, we gain valuable insights into the mechanisms of deception. This understanding not only aids in developing effective countermeasures but also informs the design of deception strategies that exploit psychological principles to enhance security. Balancing these tactics with ethical considerations ensures that cybersecurity practices remain both effective and responsible.

The interplay between psychological manipulation and deception is not merely about understanding how attackers exploit cognitive biases but also involves recognizing how these biases can be leveraged to enhance cybersecurity defenses. This deeper exploration requires a focus on the mechanisms that underpin psychological manipulation and their practical applications in both offensive and defensive strategies.

A crucial aspect of psychological manipulation is the concept of cognitive load, which refers to the amount of mental effort required to process information. Attackers often exploit cognitive load by presenting targets with complex or overwhelming information in a way that impairs their ability to think critically. For instance, a phishing email might contain multiple threats or urgent calls to action, designed to overload the recipient's cognitive processing capacity. This technique makes it more difficult for individuals to scrutinize the legitimacy of the email, increasing the likelihood of compliance with malicious requests. Understanding this manipulation allows defenders to create countermeasures that simplify and streamline information presentation, thereby reducing cognitive overload and enhancing the ability of users to identify and respond to potential threats.

Another psychological principle that plays a significant role in deception is the concept of cognitive dissonance. Cognitive dissonance occurs when an individual experiences discomfort due to conflicting beliefs or actions. Attackers can exploit this discomfort by presenting information that conflicts with the target's established beliefs or behaviors, creating a sense of urgency or self-justification. For example, an attacker might exploit cognitive dissonance by sending a message that challenges a target's understanding of their security posture, compelling them to take action to resolve the conflict, often leading to compromised security. Defenders can address cognitive dissonance by promoting consistent security practices and providing clear, coherent guidance that minimizes confusion and potential dissonance.

Understanding the role of emotional manipulation is also essential for both attackers and defenders. Emotional responses such as fear, excitement, and curiosity can significantly influence decision-making processes. Attackers frequently exploit these emotions to drive action. For instance, a common tactic is to invoke fear by suggesting imminent threats or disasters that require immediate action. This emotional manipulation can bypass rational decision-making processes and lead individuals to act impulsively. Conversely, defenders can use emotional intelligence to design deceptive strategies that capitalize on attackers' emotions, such as creating scenarios that evoke frustration or confusion. These strategies can be used to mislead attackers or lure them into traps, thereby gaining valuable insights into their tactics.

The concept of trust plays a critical role in psychological manipulation within cybersecurity. Attackers often exploit trust by impersonating trusted entities or creating fake environments that appear credible. This exploitation can be seen in various forms of attacks, including phishing, spear-phishing, and social engineering. By mimicking trusted sources, attackers can lower the target's defenses and gain access to sensitive information. Defenders can counteract this tactic by implementing robust verification mechanisms and promoting a culture of skepticism. Educating users about the importance of verifying the authenticity of communications and being cautious of unsolicited requests can help mitigate the impact of trust-based deception.

Incorporating psychological principles into defensive strategies also involves leveraging the understanding of human behavior to create effective deception. For instance, defenders can design decoy systems and fake vulnerabilities that exploit attackers' cognitive biases and emotional triggers. By creating environments that mimic real systems or simulate valuable assets, defenders can attract and trap attackers, gaining insights into their methods and intentions. The effectiveness of these deceptive measures relies on a deep understanding of attackers' psychological motivations and behaviors.

Ethical considerations remain a crucial aspect of employing psychological principles in cybersecurity. While leveraging psychological manipulation can enhance security, it is essential to ensure that these tactics are used in a manner that respects privacy, legal standards, and ethical boundaries. Defenders must carefully consider the potential impact of their deceptive strategies on legitimate users and ensure that their actions do not inadvertently cause harm or distress. Establishing clear ethical guidelines and oversight mechanisms can help balance the effectiveness of psychological tactics with the need to maintain responsible and ethical practices.

In conclusion, the application of psychological principles in cybersecurity involves a nuanced understanding of human behavior and cognitive processes. By examining how attackers exploit cognitive biases, emotional responses, and trust, we can develop effective countermeasures and deceptive strategies that enhance security. This exploration of psychological manipulation provides valuable insights into both the mechanisms of deception and the strategies for defending against it. Balancing these insights with ethical considerations ensures that cybersecurity practices remain effective, responsible, and aligned with broader organizational and societal values.

CHAPTER 3:

To fully appreciate the utility of honeypots and honeynets in cybersecurity, it is essential to explore their deployment and the insights they offer from a practical standpoint. Implementing these tools involves meticulous planning and execution to ensure that they provide meaningful data without compromising overall network security.

When setting up honeypots, one of the primary considerations is the selection of appropriate environments and services to simulate. The choice of which services to emulate should align with the organization's threat landscape and the specific objectives of the deception strategy. For instance, if an organization is concerned about attacks targeting web applications, deploying a honeypot that mimics a popular web server with known vulnerabilities would be prudent. Conversely, if the focus is on attacks against internal systems, creating a high-interaction honeypot that simulates an entire operating system or a complex database could yield more valuable insights.

The deployment of honeypots must also account for the different types of data that can be collected. Low-interaction honeypots, while simpler to deploy, provide limited interaction data. They are effective for capturing automated attacks or scanning activities but may not reveal deeper attacker intentions or techniques. High-interaction honeypots, by contrast, allow attackers to interact more fully with the system, providing richer data on their tactics and methods. However, the complexity of high-interaction honeypots requires careful management to ensure that they do not inadvertently become a liability. For example, these honeypots must be isolated from real systems to prevent any potential breach from impacting the organization's actual infrastructure.

The integration of honeypots into a broader security strategy involves considering how they fit within the existing security architecture. It is crucial to ensure that the honeypots are well monitored and that any data collected is analyzed effectively. This typically involves setting up robust logging and alerting mechanisms to track attacker interactions in real-time. Additionally, the analysis of the data collected from honeypots requires expertise in understanding attack patterns and techniques. Analysts must be adept at distinguishing between genuine threats and benign interactions, as well as interpreting the data in the context of broader threat intelligence.

Honeynets, as an extension of individual honeypots, offer an advanced level of simulation by creating a network of interconnected decoys. This setup allows for the observation of how attackers behave once they have gained access to an environment. In a honeynet, attackers might traverse multiple honeypots, potentially revealing their methods for lateral movement and privilege escalation. The complexity of a honeynet can provide insights into attack strategies that are not apparent from individual honeypots alone. For example, an attacker might first compromise a low-interaction honeypot and then attempt to move laterally to a high-interaction honeypot, demonstrating their approach to internal network exploration and data exfiltration.

The deployment of a honeynet involves additional considerations compared to single honeypots. It requires careful network design to ensure that the simulated environment accurately reflects a real network while maintaining isolation from production systems. The configuration of honeypots within the honeynet should mimic the variety of systems and services present in a typical network environment. This diversity increases the likelihood of attracting attackers with different objectives and techniques. Furthermore, managing the data from a honeynet involves coordinating the analysis of interactions across multiple honeypots, which can be complex but is critical for gaining a comprehensive understanding of attacker behavior.

In practice, honeypots and honeynets have proven effective in various real-world scenarios. One notable example involved a honeynet designed to mimic a corporate network with a range of services, including email servers, file servers, and internal applications. Attackers who accessed the honeynet were observed attempting various techniques, such as exploiting known vulnerabilities, attempting privilege escalation, and probing for sensitive information. The data collected provided insights into the attackers' methods, including their use of specific exploit tools and techniques for lateral movement. This information was invaluable for updating the organization's security posture and developing more targeted defense strategies.

Another example highlighted the use of a honeypot to investigate attacks targeting a financial institution. The honeypot, designed to emulate a banking application with vulnerabilities commonly exploited in financial fraud, captured detailed data on phishing attempts, credential stuffing attacks, and attempts to exploit application flaws. The analysis revealed patterns in the attackers' behavior, including their tactics for bypassing security measures and their use of automated tools. This intelligence informed the development of enhanced security measures and anti-fraud controls, improving the institution's ability to detect and prevent similar attacks in the future.

Despite their benefits, honeypots and honeynets are not without limitations and challenges. Managing these tools requires a balance between collecting valuable data and maintaining overall network security. The deployment of honeypots must be carefully planned to avoid inadvertently introducing vulnerabilities into the organization's infrastructure. Additionally, the data generated by these tools can be voluminous and complex, necessitating effective analysis and interpretation to extract actionable insights. It is also essential to continuously update and adapt honeypots and honeynets to address emerging threats and changes in attacker tactics.

In summary, honeypots and honeynets are powerful tools for cybersecurity deception, offering significant benefits in understanding attacker behavior and improving security defenses. Their deployment requires careful planning and management to ensure that they provide meaningful data without compromising network security. By integrating these tools into a comprehensive security strategy and analyzing the insights they provide, organizations can enhance their ability to detect, respond to, and defend against sophisticated cyber threats.

To further explore the application and impact of honeypots and honeynets, it is crucial to examine their role in various security operations and the nuances involved in their deployment and management. Understanding these aspects helps in leveraging these tools more effectively to enhance cybersecurity defenses.

When deploying honeypots and honeynets, it is essential to define clear objectives and use cases. Honeypots can be employed to achieve various goals, such as gathering information on attack methods, studying malware behavior, or identifying new vulnerabilities. By setting specific objectives, organizations can tailor their honeypot configurations to align with their security needs. For example, a honeypot might be used to track the tactics of cybercriminals targeting a particular industry, or to simulate a specific type of vulnerable application that is a known target for exploitation.

The integration of honeypots and honeynets into a security architecture requires careful consideration of several factors. One of the critical aspects is ensuring that these decoys do not inadvertently expose the network to additional risks. This involves implementing strict isolation measures to prevent any interaction between the honeypots and the organization's real systems. Proper network segmentation and firewall rules are essential to ensure that any compromise of a honeypot does not lead to an escalation of attacks within the network.

In addition to isolation, regular maintenance and updating of honeypots and honeynets are crucial. Cyber threats evolve rapidly, and attackers continuously develop new techniques and tools. To remain effective, honeypots must be updated to reflect the latest threat landscape. This may involve patching vulnerabilities, modifying the simulated environment to mirror current systems, and incorporating new types of decoys that address emerging attack vectors. Regular updates ensure that honeypots continue to attract and engage attackers, providing relevant and timely intelligence.

The analysis of data collected from honeypots and honeynets is a sophisticated process that requires expertise in threat detection and analysis. The data generated by these tools can be extensive, encompassing various types of interactions, including network traffic, command executions, and attempted exploits. Effective analysis involves filtering through this data to identify meaningful patterns and indicators of compromise. This often requires advanced analytical techniques and tools, such as machine learning algorithms and behavioral analysis, to discern between legitimate interactions and malicious activities.

One of the notable challenges in analyzing honeypot data is dealing with false positives. Since honeypots are designed to attract attackers, they may generate interactions that are not necessarily indicative of genuine threats. It is crucial to differentiate between benign activities and actual attack attempts. This involves correlating honeypot data with other sources of threat intelligence and contextual information. By cross-referencing data from multiple sources, analysts can improve the accuracy of their findings and ensure that the intelligence derived from honeypots is actionable.

The insights gained from honeypots and honeynets can significantly enhance an organization's security posture. By understanding the techniques and tactics used by attackers, security teams can develop more effective defenses. For instance, if a honeypot reveals that attackers are using a particular exploit method or tool, this information can be used to update intrusion detection systems, firewalls, and other security mechanisms to detect and block similar attacks in the future. Additionally, the intelligence gathered can inform the development of incident response plans and security policies, ensuring that the organization is better prepared to handle real-world attacks.

Case studies of honeypot and honeynet deployments provide valuable lessons on their effectiveness and potential pitfalls. For example, in a case where a honeynet was used to monitor a sophisticated cyber espionage campaign, the data collected revealed detailed information about the attackers' infrastructure, including their command and control servers and communication channels. This intelligence was instrumental in disrupting the attack and mitigating its impact. However, the deployment also highlighted the need for robust data analysis and the importance of maintaining strict isolation between honeynets and production systems.

Another example involved a honeypot designed to simulate a critical infrastructure system, such as a power grid control system. The honeypot attracted a series of targeted attacks that aimed to exploit specific vulnerabilities. The data collected provided insights into the attackers' methods for manipulating industrial control systems and highlighted vulnerabilities that were previously unknown. This information was used to strengthen the security measures protecting actual control systems and to develop better defenses against similar threats.

While honeypots and honeynets offer significant advantages, they also present challenges that must be addressed. Ensuring the security of these tools, managing the data they generate, and accurately interpreting the results require dedicated resources and expertise. Organizations must also consider the ethical implications of using honeypots, particularly in terms of privacy and legal considerations. It is essential to adhere to legal and ethical standards when deploying these tools and to ensure that they are used responsibly and in accordance with relevant regulations.

In conclusion, honeypots and honeynets are powerful tools in the realm of cybersecurity deception, providing invaluable insights into attacker behavior and enhancing defensive strategies. Their deployment and management require careful planning, ongoing maintenance, and sophisticated analysis to maximize their effectiveness. By leveraging these tools, organizations can gain a deeper understanding of cyber threats, improve their security measures, and better protect their digital assets against evolving attacks.

CHAPTER 4:

When examining the application of decoys and traps in cybersecurity, it is crucial to delve into the nuances of their implementation and effectiveness within various environments. The success of these deceptive tools largely depends on their design, deployment strategy, and the context in which they are utilized.

The deployment of decoys requires a thorough understanding of the environment in which they are placed. In a corporate setting, for example, decoys might be designed to replicate high-value assets such as financial databases or proprietary research files. The decoys must be meticulously crafted to simulate real systems, incorporating genuine operational features and vulnerabilities that would attract an attacker. This involves not only mimicking the technical aspects of these systems but also replicating their associated network traffic and user interactions. For instance, a decoy server designed to look like a financial database might need to generate typical database queries and responses to appear authentic to an attacker's reconnaissance efforts.

A critical aspect of deploying decoys is ensuring that they are appropriately integrated within the existing network infrastructure. This involves placing them in locations where they are likely to attract attention but without making them too conspicuous. The decoy systems should be positioned in such a way that they blend seamlessly with real systems, making it difficult for attackers to distinguish between genuine and deceptive assets. Network segmentation plays a pivotal role in this process, as it isolates decoy systems from critical infrastructure while still allowing them to engage potential attackers effectively.

Furthermore, the effectiveness of decoys is enhanced when they are designed with realistic and enticing attributes. This includes using accurate representations of the target environment's data, user interfaces, and operational workflows. For example, a decoy designed to simulate an email server might include fake email accounts, realistic email content, and legitimate-looking communication patterns. Such realism ensures that attackers are more likely to engage with the decoy, thereby providing valuable insights into their tactics and intentions.

In parallel, traps are an integral component of the deception strategy, designed to capture and analyze the activities of attackers who are drawn to the decoys. Traps can vary significantly in their complexity and function, ranging from simple logging mechanisms to sophisticated monitoring systems that track detailed interactions. The design of traps must be aligned with the objectives of the deception strategy, focusing on capturing relevant data that will provide actionable intelligence.

A well-designed trap might include capabilities to log every interaction with the decoy, such as file accesses, command executions, and network connections. This logging must be comprehensive to ensure that all aspects of the attack are captured. Additionally, traps can be configured to trigger alerts or automated responses when certain suspicious activities are detected. For example, if an attacker attempts to exploit a vulnerability within the decoy system, the trap could generate an alert indicating that the attack is in progress, allowing for a swift response to mitigate potential threats.

The analysis of data captured by traps requires a detailed and methodical approach. The data generated can be voluminous and complex, encompassing various types of interactions and activities. To effectively analyze this data, it is necessary to employ advanced analytical techniques and tools, such as behavioral analysis, pattern recognition, and correlation with other threat intelligence sources. This analytical process helps in identifying attack patterns, understanding the attacker's objectives, and assessing the effectiveness of the deception strategy.

Real-world examples illustrate the practical applications and benefits of decoys and traps. In one case, a healthcare organization deployed a series of decoy systems designed to mimic patient records and medical databases. These decoys were integrated into the network alongside real systems, creating a convincing environment for potential attackers. The associated traps monitored interactions with the decoys, capturing detailed information about attempted breaches and data exfiltration activities. The insights gained from this data enabled the organization to strengthen its defenses and improve its response strategies to real-world threats.

Another example involved a technology company that used decoys to protect its intellectual property. The company created decoy systems that replicated the design and functionality of its proprietary software. By luring attackers to these decoys, the company was able to monitor their attempts to access and exploit the simulated software. The traps employed captured detailed logs of the attackers' actions, including their methods for bypassing security controls and their attempts to reverse-engineer the decoy software. This information was invaluable in enhancing the company's security measures and preventing actual breaches of its intellectual property.

While decoys and traps offer significant advantages in cybersecurity, their implementation must be approached with careful consideration of potential challenges. Ensuring the accuracy and effectiveness of decoys requires ongoing maintenance and updates to reflect evolving threats and attack methods. Similarly, the data captured by traps must be analyzed diligently to extract meaningful insights and address any false positives or irrelevant information.

Additionally, the ethical and legal implications of using deception tools must be considered. Organizations must ensure that their use of decoys and traps complies with relevant regulations and privacy standards. This includes ensuring that deceptive practices do not infringe on individuals' rights or expose sensitive information inadvertently.

In conclusion, the strategic use of decoys and traps in cybersecurity provides valuable methods for attracting, capturing, and analyzing attacker activities. By designing and deploying these tools effectively, organizations can gain critical insights into cyber threats, enhance their defensive capabilities, and better protect their valuable assets. The implementation of decoys and traps requires careful planning, ongoing maintenance, and rigorous analysis to maximize their effectiveness and ensure their alignment with overall security objectives.

The effectiveness of decoys and traps is significantly influenced by their integration into broader security frameworks and the strategic alignment with organizational objectives. To maximize their utility, it is essential to consider how these deceptive tools complement existing security measures and contribute to a comprehensive defense strategy.

Decoys must be designed with a clear understanding of the potential threat landscape and the specific tactics used by attackers. This involves not only creating realistic simulations of valuable assets but also anticipating the likely methods attackers will use to probe and exploit these decoys. For example, if an organization is known to be a target for ransomware attacks, decoys should include elements that mimic valuable data repositories and operational systems that ransomware would typically aim to encrypt or exfiltrate. The decoy environment should reflect the same configurations, access permissions, and data types that an attacker might expect in a real-world scenario. This level of detail ensures that attackers are drawn to the decoys and engage with them as they would with genuine systems.

Moreover, effective deployment of decoys requires continuous monitoring and adaptation. Attackers constantly evolve their techniques, so decoys must be updated to reflect current threat trends. Regular updates to the decoy environment, including the introduction of new data and the simulation of emerging attack vectors, help maintain the relevance of decoys and ensure they continue to attract attackers. This process also involves periodic review and adjustment of the decoy's configuration to address any weaknesses that could be exploited or any new vulnerabilities that might emerge.

The integration of traps within a decoy environment is equally critical. Traps are not standalone tools but rather components of a holistic deception strategy. They need to be strategically placed within the decoy environment to capture relevant information without interfering with legitimate operations. For instance, a trap might be positioned to monitor interactions with a specific part of a decoy's network, such as a faux financial application, to gather detailed logs of unauthorized access attempts or data manipulation efforts. The data collected by these traps can then be analyzed to gain insights into attacker behavior, including their tactics, techniques, and procedures.

To ensure that traps are effective, they must be equipped with robust monitoring and logging capabilities. This includes capturing a comprehensive set of data points, such as network traffic, system logs, and user interactions. Advanced analytics tools can then be used to process this data, providing a clearer picture of the attacker's actions and intentions. For instance, analyzing patterns in network traffic might reveal attempts to exfiltrate data or bypass security controls, offering valuable intelligence that can inform subsequent defensive measures.

Real-world scenarios underscore the importance of integrating decoys and traps within a broader security strategy. In one instance, a government agency facing persistent cyber threats deployed a network of decoys designed to simulate high-value national security assets. These decoys were embedded within a complex network environment, complete with fake communications and operational data. The associated traps monitored interactions with the decoys, capturing detailed information about attempted intrusions and the techniques used by attackers. This intelligence provided critical insights into the nature of the threats faced by the agency and enabled the development of more targeted and effective defense strategies.

Another example involves a technology firm that used decoys and traps to protect intellectual property. The firm deployed decoys designed to mimic the company's proprietary software and research data. Traps within these decoys captured detailed logs of interactions, including attempts to reverse-engineer the software or access protected research. The information gathered from these traps allowed the firm to identify potential vulnerabilities in its real systems and to strengthen its security posture against similar attack methods.

While the implementation of decoys and traps can offer substantial benefits, organizations must also consider the potential challenges and limitations associated with their use. One challenge is ensuring that decoys and traps do not inadvertently interfere with legitimate operations or compromise sensitive data. Proper isolation and segregation of decoy environments from real systems are essential to mitigate this risk. Additionally, organizations must be prepared to manage and analyze large volumes of data generated by traps, which requires specialized tools and expertise.

Legal and ethical considerations also play a crucial role in the deployment of decoys and traps. Organizations must ensure that their use of deceptive techniques complies with relevant laws and regulations, including those related to privacy and data protection. It is essential to use these tools responsibly and transparently, balancing the need for effective security with the rights and expectations of individuals and stakeholders.

In conclusion, the strategic use of decoys and traps in cybersecurity provides powerful methods for attracting, capturing, and analyzing attacker activities. By integrating these tools into a broader security framework and continuously adapting them to address evolving threats, organizations can enhance their ability to protect sensitive information and detect malicious activities. The successful deployment of decoys and traps requires careful planning, ongoing maintenance, and rigorous analysis to maximize their effectiveness and ensure alignment with overall security objectives.

CHAPTER 5:

Creating fake data and false flags within cybersecurity environments involves intricate strategies designed to mislead and manipulate attackers, thereby enhancing the protection of sensitive assets. By implementing these tactics, organizations can introduce layers of confusion that obscure the true nature of their systems and misdirect adversaries. This process requires a nuanced understanding of both data manipulation and deceptive signaling, ensuring that the methods employed are both effective and aligned with the organization's overall security strategy.

The deployment of fake data is not a mere act of generating irrelevant information but a deliberate process of creating realistic and believable datasets that can deceive attackers into believing they have accessed genuine information. This often involves constructing data that mirrors the structure and content of critical assets but is ultimately devoid of real value. The creation of such data must be meticulous; it requires an understanding of the typical data patterns and structures that attackers expect to encounter. For instance, if an attacker is targeting financial systems, the fake data should include realistic transaction records, account details, and financial summaries that reflect common industry practices.

One effective approach to creating convincing fake data is to use data generators and simulators that can produce large volumes of data with varying degrees of complexity. These tools can be configured to generate data that mimics the characteristics of real operational data, including trends, anomalies, and usage patterns. The goal is to craft data sets that not only appear authentic but also interact with the system in ways that replicate legitimate usage scenarios. This increases the likelihood that attackers will engage with the fake data, thereby diverting their focus from actual, sensitive information.

Additionally, integrating fake data into live environments presents a unique set of challenges and opportunities. To maintain the effectiveness of fake data, it must be seamlessly incorporated into the operational data streams, ensuring that it blends with the genuine data without causing disruptions. This integration often involves employing sophisticated data masking techniques to obscure real data while presenting fake data in a manner that appears natural. This helps to ensure that attackers do not easily distinguish between real and fake data, further enhancing the deception.

The concept of false flags complements the use of fake data by introducing misleading signals that misrepresent the origins or nature of an attack. False flags can be used to create confusion regarding the source of an attack, potentially misdirecting forensic investigations and response efforts. This involves manipulating evidence or creating deliberate misdirection to suggest that an attack is originating from a different source or is being executed with different intentions than it actually is.

For example, an organization might use false flags by planting malware with attributes or signatures that resemble those used by a known adversary. This can lead the security team or incident responders to attribute the attack to that particular threat actor, thereby diverting their focus and resources away from the actual source. In some cases, false flags can also involve creating misleading traces in network traffic or log files that mimic the patterns of other threat actors, adding another layer of complexity to the attribution process.

Another approach to employing false flags involves creating

misleading operational patterns that suggest an attack is targeting a different set of assets or utilizing different attack vectors. This can be achieved by introducing anomalies or suspicious activities that align with known tactics of other threat actors, thereby causing confusion and misdirecting the attacker's efforts. By making the attack appear to be part of a different campaign or strategy, organizations can gain valuable time to fortify their defenses and prepare more effective countermeasures.

Implementing fake data and false flags requires careful planning and execution to ensure that the deception does not inadvertently expose or compromise genuine assets. The creation of fake data must be done with a clear understanding of the data environment and the potential impact on operational systems. Similarly, false flags must be designed to be convincing yet not so disruptive that they interfere with normal operations or create unintended vulnerabilities.

Practical examples of these techniques illustrate their effectiveness in real-world scenarios. In one instance, a healthcare organization under constant threat from cybercriminals employed fake data to protect patient records. The organization created a series of decoy databases containing fake patient information and integrated them into their network. When attackers attempted to access these databases, they were met with realistic yet worthless data that led them away from the actual patient records. This approach not only safeguarded sensitive information but also provided insights into the attackers' methods and motives.

In another case, a government agency targeted by sophisticated adversaries used false flags to mislead the attackers about their network's configuration and vulnerabilities. By introducing misleading indicators and artifacts that suggested the presence of different security technologies and defenses, the agency successfully created a false sense of security for the attackers.

This strategy allowed the agency to better understand the attackers' tactics and adapt their defensive measures accordingly.

In summary, the strategic use of fake data and false flags in cybersecurity provides powerful tools for deception and protection. By crafting convincing fake datasets and introducing misleading signals, organizations can effectively confuse and mislead attackers, protecting critical assets and gaining a strategic advantage. The successful implementation of these techniques requires a deep understanding of the data environment, careful planning, and precise execution to ensure that the deception aligns with the organization's overall security objectives.

When implementing fake data and false flags, it is crucial to consider the potential impact on the broader security landscape and the effectiveness of the deceptive measures. The key to success in utilizing these techniques lies in their integration with the overall cybersecurity strategy, ensuring that they complement other defensive measures and enhance the organization's ability to thwart and understand cyber threats.

The creation of fake data involves not only generating believable datasets but also embedding them within a realistic context that mirrors the operational environment. This means that fake data must be continuously updated and maintained to reflect changes in the system's actual data. For instance, if an organization's real-time transaction records are subject to frequent updates, the fake data should also be periodically refreshed to maintain its credibility. This dynamic approach helps ensure that attackers do not easily discern between genuine and deceptive data, thereby increasing the effectiveness of the diversion.

Another important aspect of using fake data is ensuring that it is designed to interact with potential attack vectors in a way that aligns with real data patterns. This requires an in-depth understanding of how attackers typically probe and exploit systems. By analyzing common attack behaviors and strategies, organizations can tailor their fake data to simulate realistic scenarios that are likely to attract and engage adversaries. This tailored approach ensures that attackers are drawn to the fake data and invest time and resources in it, thereby reducing the risk to actual critical information.

In parallel, the use of false flags involves creating misleading signals that suggest incorrect attack vectors or sources. To implement this effectively, it is necessary to design and deploy false flags in a manner that convincingly aligns with known threat actor behaviors or attack techniques. For example, if an organization suspects that attackers are targeting specific vulnerabilities associated with a particular malware strain, introducing false indicators that suggest the presence of that malware can mislead attackers and redirect their efforts. This approach can be particularly useful in scenarios where the organization wants to protect specific high-value assets or anticipate potential future attacks based on current intelligence.

False flags can also be used to manipulate the attack narrative and influence the response strategies of adversaries. By creating misleading indicators, organizations can cause attackers to overestimate the complexity or scale of the defense mechanisms in place. This misdirection can lead attackers to alter their tactics or abandon their efforts altogether, providing the organization with critical time to strengthen its defenses or mount an effective counterattack.

However, the deployment of false flags must be handled with caution to avoid unintended consequences. If false flags are too elaborate or poorly executed, they can inadvertently create confusion within the organization or mislead incident responders. This risk underscores the importance of carefully planning and coordinating the use of false flags to ensure that they achieve the desired effect without introducing additional vulnerabilities or complications.

Moreover, the effectiveness of fake data and false flags depends on continuous monitoring and evaluation. Organizations must regularly assess the performance of their deceptive measures and adjust their strategies based on emerging threat intelligence and attack patterns. This ongoing evaluation helps ensure that fake data and false flags remain relevant and effective in countering evolving threats.

Real-world examples illustrate the successful application of these techniques in various contexts. In one notable case, a financial institution under persistent threat from cybercriminals used fake data to protect its core financial systems. By embedding decoy transaction records and account details into its network, the institution successfully diverted attackers' attention from actual sensitive data. This not only protected critical financial information but also provided valuable insights into the attackers' methods and motivations.

In another instance, a technology company facing sophisticated state-sponsored attacks employed false flags to mislead adversaries about the organization's internal security posture. By creating misleading indicators that suggested the presence of advanced security technologies and defensive measures, the company caused attackers to reassess their strategies and focus on less critical targets. This approach allowed the company to better understand the attackers' tactics and develop more effective countermeasures.

The strategic use of fake data and false flags highlights the importance of deception in modern cybersecurity practices. By leveraging these techniques, organizations can create a deceptive environment that confuses and misleads attackers, thereby enhancing their ability to protect critical assets and respond effectively to cyber threats. The key to successful implementation lies in careful planning, continuous monitoring, and alignment with the overall security strategy, ensuring that deceptive measures effectively complement and strengthen the organization's defensive capabilities.

Ultimately, the goal of using fake data and false flags is to create a robust and dynamic security posture that not only protects against current threats but also anticipates and mitigates future risks. By integrating these techniques into a comprehensive cybersecurity strategy, organizations can enhance their ability to detect, respond to, and ultimately prevent malicious activities, ensuring the continued protection of their valuable assets and information.

CHAPTER 6:

To create a deceptive network architecture effectively, it is essential to implement several advanced techniques beyond basic segmentation, false endpoints, and simulated services. These techniques include deploying dynamic decoys, integrating with threat intelligence, and ensuring that deception elements blend seamlessly with genuine network components. By employing these advanced methods, an organization can enhance its ability to mislead attackers and gather actionable intelligence.

Dynamic decoys are an evolution of static false endpoints and simulate the behavior of real systems that are constantly changing. Unlike static decoys, which remain fixed and predictable, dynamic decoys adapt their behavior based on the interactions they encounter. This dynamic nature helps in maintaining the illusion of authenticity, making it more difficult for attackers to distinguish between genuine and deceptive elements. For instance, a dynamic decoy might simulate fluctuations in network traffic, alter its responses based on the attacker's actions, or even change its configuration over time to mimic the evolving nature of a real system. This adaptability increases the likelihood of engaging attackers and capturing more detailed insights into their tactics.

The integration of deceptive network elements with threat intelligence further amplifies the effectiveness of a deceptive network architecture. Threat intelligence provides valuable context about emerging threats, attack patterns, and known adversaries. By incorporating this information into the design and operation of deceptive elements, organizations can create more realistic and relevant traps for attackers. For example, if threat intelligence reveals that a particular type of malware is targeting specific vulnerabilities, the deceptive network can be updated to include simulated vulnerabilities that mimic these threats. This integration ensures that deceptive measures remain current and aligned with the latest threat landscape, enhancing their ability to deceive and detect malicious activities.

Another crucial aspect of implementing deceptive network architectures is ensuring that deception elements are indistinguishable from legitimate network components. This requires a thorough understanding of the organization's actual network environment and the creation of deception elements that closely mimic genuine systems. For instance, simulated services and decoys must be configured to replicate real network traffic patterns, user interactions, and system behaviors. This level of realism helps prevent attackers from recognizing deceptive elements and enables them to engage more deeply with the traps set for them. The key is to create a network environment where the boundaries between genuine and deceptive elements are blurred, making it challenging for attackers to differentiate between the two.

Effective management of deceptive network architectures also involves regular updates and maintenance of deceptive elements. As an organization's network evolves and new threats emerge, the deceptive components must be adjusted to reflect these changes. This includes refreshing dynamic decoys, updating simulated services to mimic new vulnerabilities or attack methods, and modifying network segmentation as needed. Ongoing monitoring and analysis of attacker interactions with deceptive elements provide valuable feedback that can inform these updates. By continuously refining and adapting the deceptive network, organizations can ensure that their defensive measures remain effective and relevant.

In addition to these technical considerations, it is essential to evaluate the legal and ethical implications of deploying deceptive network architectures. Organizations must navigate legal and regulatory requirements related to cybersecurity and data protection while implementing deceptive measures. This involves ensuring that deceptive tactics do not inadvertently violate privacy laws, breach data protection regulations, or cause harm to legitimate users. It is crucial to establish clear policies and guidelines for the use of deception in the network environment and to engage with legal and compliance experts to address any potential issues.

One illustrative case study involves a multinational corporation that faced a sophisticated and persistent threat actor targeting its intellectual property. To counter this threat, the corporation implemented a deceptive network architecture that included dynamic decoys and simulated services designed to mimic its proprietary research and development environments. By integrating threat intelligence into the design of these deceptive elements, the corporation was able to create highly realistic traps that attracted the attacker. The dynamic nature of the decoys allowed the organization to capture detailed information about the attacker's tactics and techniques, leading to the identification of previously unknown attack vectors and the development of targeted defensive measures.

Another example is a government agency tasked with protecting critical infrastructure from advanced persistent threats. The agency employed a deceptive network architecture to create a layered defense strategy, incorporating both static and dynamic deceptive elements. This approach included false endpoints that simulated essential infrastructure components, as well as simulated services that mimicked the agency's operational systems. By closely monitoring interactions with these deceptive elements, the agency was able to detect and respond to threats in real time, gaining valuable insights into the attackers' methods and improving its overall security posture.

In summary, designing and implementing deceptive network architectures involves a range of advanced techniques and considerations. By incorporating dynamic decoys, integrating with threat intelligence, and ensuring that deceptive elements closely mimic genuine systems, organizations can create effective and realistic environments that deceive and trap attackers. Ongoing management and adaptation of these deceptive measures, along with careful attention to legal and ethical considerations, are essential for maximizing their effectiveness and ensuring their alignment with organizational goals and regulatory requirements.

Building on the foundational concepts of deceptive network architectures, it is crucial to delve into the more nuanced aspects of their deployment, specifically focusing on the interaction between deceptive and genuine network elements. A sophisticated deceptive network architecture not only integrates deceptive elements seamlessly with real systems but also involves intricate coordination to ensure that these elements effectively capture and analyze attacker behavior without compromising legitimate operations.

One advanced technique in deceptive network design involves creating interactive traps that engage attackers in complex scenarios. These traps go beyond static decoys by providing a dynamic environment that mimics real-world systems and responses. For instance, a deceptive trap might include simulated user interfaces, interactive applications, or even fake database queries that respond in real-time to the attacker's actions. This level of interaction increases the likelihood of capturing detailed and actionable intelligence about the attacker's methods, tools, and objectives. By engaging attackers in a more immersive and responsive environment, organizations can gain deeper insights into their strategies and improve their defensive measures.

Another critical aspect is the integration of deceptive network components with existing security systems, such as intrusion detection systems (IDS) and security information and event management (SIEM) platforms. Effective integration ensures that deceptive elements do not operate in isolation but rather contribute to a comprehensive security strategy. For example, when an attacker interacts with a deceptive element, the activity should be logged and analyzed by the organization's SIEM system. This integration allows for real-time correlation of deceptive activities with other security events, providing a holistic view of the threat landscape. Additionally, integrating deceptive components with IDS can enhance their ability to detect and respond to sophisticated attacks, as these systems can be configured to recognize and analyze patterns associated with deceptive elements.

A further consideration in deploying deceptive network architectures is the management of false positives and the potential for interference with legitimate operations. As deceptive elements become more complex and integrated with real systems, there is a risk that legitimate activities might be misclassified as malicious or that deceptive traps might inadvertently disrupt normal operations. To mitigate this risk, it is essential to implement rigorous monitoring and validation processes to distinguish between genuine and deceptive events. Regular testing and tuning of deceptive elements are necessary to ensure that they do not generate excessive false positives or interfere with legitimate user activities. This ongoing management helps maintain the effectiveness of the deceptive network while minimizing potential disruptions.

In addition to technical considerations, organizational policies and procedures play a vital role in the successful deployment of deceptive network architectures. Establishing clear guidelines for the use of deceptive elements, defining roles and responsibilities, and ensuring compliance with legal and regulatory requirements are essential components of a robust deception strategy. Organizations must develop and implement policies that govern the deployment, management, and monitoring of deceptive components, including protocols for responding to detected threats and handling incidents. These policies should also address the ethical implications of using deception in cybersecurity, ensuring that deceptive tactics are employed responsibly and transparently.

A compelling example of advanced deceptive network architecture can be found in a financial institution that sought to protect its sensitive financial data from sophisticated attackers. The institution implemented a network design incorporating both static and dynamic deceptive elements, including simulated trading systems, fake customer accounts, and interactive traps. These elements were carefully integrated with the organization's real systems and security infrastructure, providing a seamless environment for detecting and analyzing attacks. By closely monitoring interactions with the deceptive elements and analyzing the captured data, the institution was able to identify new attack vectors and refine its security posture accordingly. The integration of deceptive components with the institution's IDS and SIEM systems allowed for real-time detection and response, enhancing the overall effectiveness of its security strategy.

Another illustrative case involves a technology company that used deceptive network architectures to protect its intellectual property from targeted cyber espionage. The company created a sophisticated network environment with multiple layers of deception, including false endpoints, simulated services, and dynamic decoys. The deceptive elements were designed to mimic the company's real development and research environments, making it challenging for attackers to discern genuine from deceptive assets. By analyzing interactions with these deceptive components, the company was able to gather valuable intelligence on the tactics and techniques employed by the attackers. This intelligence informed the company's defensive strategies, leading to improved protection of its critical intellectual property.

In summary, the effective design and implementation of deceptive network architectures require a multifaceted approach that encompasses advanced techniques, integration with existing security systems, and careful management of potential risks. By creating interactive traps, integrating with IDS and SIEM platforms, and establishing robust organizational policies, organizations can enhance their ability to detect, analyze, and respond to cyber threats. The case studies provided illustrate how deceptive network architectures can be leveraged to protect sensitive information and disrupt attacker strategies, demonstrating the practical value of these approaches in real-world scenarios.

CHAPTER 7:

When integrating behavioral analytics with deception techniques, it is crucial to understand how data from user and attacker interactions can be used to enhance the effectiveness of deceptive strategies. Behavioral analytics provides a detailed view into the normal and anomalous behavior patterns within a network, allowing us to tailor deceptive elements to be more engaging and revealing.

Behavioral analytics relies heavily on continuous monitoring to detect deviations from established norms. By examining the patterns in user activities, organizations can establish a baseline of what constitutes normal behavior. For example, in a corporate environment, this might include typical login times, data access patterns, or communication frequencies. Once this baseline is established, any significant deviation—such as an unusual login attempt during off-hours or from an atypical location—can be flagged as potentially suspicious. This is where machine learning algorithms come into play. These algorithms analyze vast quantities of data, learning from historical interactions to recognize subtle anomalies that might indicate a threat.

Machine learning models used in behavioral analytics are designed to identify and predict deviations based on a combination of statistical methods and historical data. Supervised learning algorithms, for example, are trained on labeled datasets that contain known examples of both normal and malicious behavior. Through this training, the model learns to differentiate between the two and can then apply this knowledge to identify similar patterns in new data. Unsupervised learning algorithms, on the other hand, work without predefined labels, seeking out patterns and anomalies that do not fit the established norms. Both approaches are valuable for detecting sophisticated attacks that might evade simpler detection methods.

Integrating these insights with deception techniques involves using the knowledge gained from behavioral analytics to inform the design and deployment of deceptive elements. For instance, if analytics reveal that attackers often target specific types of data or systems, we can create deceptive environments that mimic these high-value targets. By aligning the deceptive elements with the behavior patterns observed, organizations can increase the likelihood of capturing detailed information about the attackers' methods and objectives.

One effective strategy for incorporating behavioral analytics into deceptive practices is the use of adaptive decoys. These decoys are dynamic, changing based on the real-time data provided by behavioral analytics. If an attacker interacts with a decoy that appears to be a high-value asset, the system can adjust its responses or introduce additional deceptive elements to better engage and capture the attacker. This adaptability ensures that the deceptive elements remain relevant and effective, even as the attacker's tactics evolve.

Another crucial aspect is the implementation of real-time feedback mechanisms. As attackers interact with deceptive elements, behavioral analytics can provide ongoing insights into their actions. This real-time data allows for immediate adjustments to the deception strategy, enhancing its ability to capture and analyze the attacker's behavior. For example, if an attacker shows interest in a particular type of data or system, the deceptive environment can be modified to include more of these elements, thereby increasing the chances of capturing valuable information.

Additionally, behavioral analytics can help in monitoring the effectiveness of deceptive strategies. By analyzing how attackers interact with deceptive elements, organizations can gain insights into which tactics are most successful and identify areas for improvement. This iterative process of analyzing and refining deceptive practices ensures that they remain effective in addressing emerging threats.

Real-world applications of this integration can be observed in various case studies. For example, consider a security operation that uses behavioral analytics to monitor for unusual login patterns. By integrating this data with a deceptive environment designed to simulate sensitive financial systems, the organization can create a dynamic and engaging trap for potential attackers. The behavioral analytics data can then be used to adjust the deceptive elements in real-time, enhancing their effectiveness and providing valuable insights into the attackers' methods.

In another scenario, a technology company may use behavioral analytics to detect deviations in network traffic patterns. By incorporating deceptive network segments that simulate critical infrastructure, the company can attract attackers and observe their behavior. The data gathered from these interactions, combined with insights from behavioral analytics, can inform further refinements to the deceptive strategies, improving the company's overall security posture.

In conclusion, the integration of behavioral analytics with deception techniques represents a powerful approach to enhancing cybersecurity defenses. By leveraging the insights gained from monitoring and analyzing user and attacker behavior, organizations can create more effective and adaptive deceptive environments. Machine learning algorithms play a critical role in identifying anomalous patterns, while real-time feedback and iterative refinement ensure that deceptive strategies remain relevant and effective. Through practical applications and case studies, we see how this integration can provide a robust defense against sophisticated attacks, offering a more comprehensive approach to cybersecurity.

In considering the practical deployment of behavioral analytics within deception frameworks, it becomes apparent that continuous adaptation is crucial for maintaining effectiveness. The fusion of behavioral analytics with deceptive techniques not only heightens the detection and response capabilities but also facilitates a more proactive approach to cybersecurity. This synergy allows for a more nuanced understanding of attack vectors and attacker behavior, ultimately leading to a more resilient defense posture.

One of the core elements in integrating behavioral analytics with deceptive techniques is the establishment of a comprehensive monitoring system. This system should be capable of capturing a wide range of data from various sources, including network traffic, user interactions, and system logs. The depth and breadth of data collected play a vital role in accurately analyzing behavior and identifying deviations from the norm. It is imperative that the monitoring system is configured to handle large volumes of data and can provide timely insights into potential threats.

The use of machine learning algorithms is particularly advantageous in this context. These algorithms can be employed to process and analyze the data collected from various sources, identifying patterns that might be indicative of malicious activity. Supervised learning models, which rely on pre-labeled datasets, can be trained to recognize specific types of attacks or suspicious behavior based on historical data. This training enables the model to detect similar patterns in new data, providing early warnings of potential threats.

Conversely, unsupervised learning models are beneficial for identifying novel or previously unknown attack patterns. These models analyze data without predefined labels, seeking out anomalies and outliers that deviate from established norms. In a deceptive network environment, unsupervised learning can reveal new tactics employed by attackers and help refine the deceptive elements to address these emerging threats.

Behavioral analytics also facilitates the creation of adaptive deception strategies. By continuously analyzing user and attacker behavior, organizations can adjust the deceptive elements in real-time to enhance their effectiveness. For instance, if an attacker demonstrates a preference for a specific type of data or system, the deceptive environment can be modified to include more of these elements. This dynamic adjustment ensures that the deceptive tactics remain relevant and engaging, increasing the likelihood of capturing valuable information about the attacker's methods and intentions.

The integration of behavioral analytics into deception strategies also involves setting up feedback loops that allow for real-time adjustments. As attackers interact with deceptive elements, their behavior can be monitored and analyzed to provide immediate insights into their tactics. This real-time data can inform adjustments to the deceptive environment, ensuring that it remains effective in luring and capturing attackers. Feedback loops not only enhance the effectiveness of deception but also contribute to a more agile and responsive security posture.

Case studies highlight the practical applications of integrating behavioral analytics with deception. For example, a financial institution might use behavioral analytics to monitor for unusual access patterns within its network. By deploying deceptive elements that simulate sensitive financial data, the institution can attract attackers and observe their behavior. The insights gained from analyzing the attackers' interactions with these decoys can then be used to refine the deception strategy and improve overall security measures.

Similarly, a technology company may implement behavioral analytics to detect deviations in network traffic that could indicate a potential attack. By setting up deceptive network segments that mimic critical infrastructure, the company can attract and monitor attackers. The data gathered from these interactions, combined with behavioral insights, can inform further refinements to the deceptive environment, enhancing its ability to detect and respond to sophisticated attacks.

Moreover, the combination of behavioral analytics with deception provides valuable insights into attacker motivations and objectives. By analyzing how attackers interact with deceptive elements, organizations can gain a deeper understanding of their targets and methods. This knowledge can inform the development of more targeted and effective security measures, addressing specific weaknesses and improving overall defense strategies.

In summary, the integration of behavioral analytics with deception techniques represents a powerful approach to enhancing cybersecurity defenses. By leveraging the insights gained from monitoring and analyzing behavior, organizations can create more effective and adaptive deceptive environments. Machine learning algorithms play a crucial role in identifying anomalies and refining deceptive tactics, while real-time feedback mechanisms ensure that the deception remains relevant and effective. Through practical applications and case studies, it is evident that this integration provides a robust defense against sophisticated attacks, offering a comprehensive and agile approach to modern cybersecurity challenges.

CHAPTER 8:

Deception techniques in cloud environments leverage the inherent flexibility and scalability of cloud computing to create dynamic and adaptive security measures. The integration of deception into cloud environments introduces a range of sophisticated strategies that can enhance an organization's ability to detect, analyze, and respond to cyber threats effectively. One of the core elements of this integration is the deployment of virtual honeypots.

Virtual honeypots in cloud environments are distinct from traditional honeypots due to their ability to be rapidly provisioned, scaled, and decommissioned in response to evolving threats. The ephemeral nature of cloud resources allows for the creation of honeypots that closely mimic real cloud-based services and applications. By simulating various components such as virtual machines, storage systems, and databases, organizations can craft convincing environments that entice attackers into interacting with deceptive assets. The advantage of using virtual honeypots in the cloud is their ability to blend seamlessly with legitimate cloud infrastructure, making it challenging for attackers to distinguish between real and deceptive elements.

The deployment of cloud-based decoys represents another crucial strategy in the realm of deception within cloud environments. Cloud-based decoys are designed to replicate real cloud services and applications, creating an illusion of valuable targets for attackers. These decoys can be configured to appear as critical business systems or sensitive data repositories, drawing attackers into a controlled and monitored environment. For example, a cloud-based decoy may be designed to mimic a financial database, complete with realistic-looking data and access controls. When attackers attempt to interact with this decoy, their actions can be closely observed, analyzed, and used to gain insights into their methods and objectives.

Managing deceptive assets in multi-tenant cloud environments adds a layer of complexity to the implementation of deception techniques. Multi-tenant environments are characterized by the sharing of physical infrastructure among multiple customers, which necessitates strict isolation of resources to prevent cross-tenant data leakage or interference. To address this challenge, organizations must ensure that deceptive assets are carefully segregated from legitimate resources. This involves employing advanced isolation techniques and leveraging cloud provider features that enforce tenant separation. For instance, implementing network segmentation and virtual private clouds (VPCs) can help to create distinct network zones for deceptive assets, preventing unauthorized access or contamination.

The dynamic and scalable nature of cloud environments also impacts the management and orchestration of deceptive elements. Cloud resources can be rapidly allocated and retracted based on demand, and this agility must be reflected in the deployment of deceptive assets. Automation plays a pivotal role in this process, allowing organizations to deploy, configure, and decommission deceptive resources in an efficient and timely manner. Automation tools and orchestration platforms can be used to manage the lifecycle of deceptive assets, ensuring that they are consistently maintained and aligned with the current threat landscape.

Additionally, integrating cloud-native security features into deceptive strategies enhances their effectiveness. Cloud providers offer a range of built-in security services that can support and augment deception techniques. For example, cloud-based threat detection and monitoring services can be utilized to gain visibility into potential attacker activities within deceptive environments. These services often leverage machine learning and behavioral analytics to identify anomalies and suspicious patterns, providing valuable insights into attacker behavior. By combining these cloud-native capabilities with deception techniques, organizations can achieve a more comprehensive and proactive approach to threat detection.

Incorporating behavioral analytics into the management of deceptive assets further strengthens their role in cloud environments. Behavioral analytics involves the use of machine learning algorithms to analyze patterns of user and attacker behavior, identifying deviations from established norms. When applied to deceptive environments, behavioral analytics can help to discern between legitimate interactions and potential threats, improving the accuracy of threat detection and response. For example, anomalous behavior detected within a cloud-based decoy can prompt automated alerts and responses, allowing for a swift and coordinated reaction to potential attacks.

Finally, organizations must consider the legal and compliance implications of deploying deception in cloud environments. The use of deceptive techniques must align with regulatory requirements and industry standards, ensuring that privacy and data protection considerations are addressed. This may involve implementing measures to ensure that deceptive assets do not inadvertently expose sensitive or personal data, and that any monitoring or analysis of attacker behavior is conducted in accordance with relevant legal frameworks.

In summary, the deployment of deception techniques in cloud environments requires a nuanced and adaptive approach that leverages the unique characteristics of cloud computing. Virtual honeypots and cloud-based decoys offer powerful tools for creating deceptive landscapes that attract and trap attackers, while the management of deceptive assets in multi-tenant environments necessitates careful attention to isolation and access controls. By integrating automation, cloud-native security features, and behavioral analytics into deception strategies, organizations can enhance their ability to detect and respond to sophisticated threats, achieving a more resilient and effective cybersecurity posture.

The integration of deception strategies into cloud environments not only requires a deep understanding of cloud computing principles but also demands an approach tailored to the nuances and complexities of cloud infrastructures. One of the foremost considerations in deploying deception in such environments is ensuring that deceptive techniques do not inadvertently disrupt legitimate operations or expose sensitive information. This necessitates a strategic and carefully orchestrated implementation of deceptive elements.

In a cloud environment, the scale and dynamism of resources present unique opportunities for creating sophisticated deceptive frameworks. For instance, one effective approach involves the use of dynamic decoy instances that can be spun up and down on demand. This dynamic nature allows for the creation of deceptive environments that can evolve in real-time based on the activities observed. By leveraging cloud orchestration tools, organizations can automate the deployment of these decoys, ensuring that they are activated in response to specific threat indicators or behavioral anomalies.

Moreover, the use of cloud-native services and infrastructure to support deceptive strategies enhances their effectiveness. Cloud providers offer a variety of managed services, such as serverless computing and container orchestration, which can be employed to create highly adaptable and scalable deceptive environments. Serverless computing, for example, allows for the creation of functions that can be executed in response to specific triggers, making it possible to deploy deceptive elements that are activated only when certain conditions are met. This not only optimizes resource utilization but also minimizes the risk of exposing deceptive assets unnecessarily.

Containerization is another critical technology in the context of cloud-based deception. Containers can encapsulate deceptive services or applications, providing a lightweight and isolated environment that can be easily managed and scaled. By using container orchestration platforms like Kubernetes, organizations can deploy and manage large numbers of containers that simulate a variety of services and applications, creating a comprehensive and convincing deceptive landscape. This approach also enables rapid redeployment of deceptive assets, ensuring that they remain relevant and effective against evolving threats.

Managing deceptive assets in multi-tenant cloud environments requires a robust approach to security and isolation. Multi-tenancy introduces the risk of cross-tenant data leakage or interference, which can compromise both legitimate operations and deceptive measures. To mitigate these risks, it is essential to implement stringent access controls and isolation mechanisms. Virtual private clouds (VPCs) and network segmentation play a crucial role in ensuring that deceptive assets are effectively isolated from other tenants and from critical infrastructure. Additionally, employing encryption for data at rest and in transit adds an extra layer of protection, ensuring that any deceptive data remains secure and segregated.

Incorporating deception into cloud environments also necessitates a consideration of compliance and legal requirements. Organizations must ensure that their deceptive practices adhere to relevant regulations and standards, particularly with regard to data privacy and protection. This may involve implementing measures to ensure that deceptive assets do not inadvertently expose personal or sensitive data, and that any monitoring or analysis of attacker activities is conducted in a manner that respects privacy rights. It is also crucial to maintain transparency and accountability in the deployment of deceptive techniques, documenting their use and ensuring that they are aligned with organizational policies and legal frameworks.

Another key aspect of deploying deception in cloud environments is the integration of behavioral analytics. Behavioral analytics enhances the effectiveness of deception by providing deeper insights into attacker behavior and interactions with deceptive assets. By analyzing patterns of activity and identifying deviations from normal behavior, organizations can gain a better understanding of how attackers operate and tailor their deceptive measures accordingly. Machine learning algorithms can play a pivotal role in this process, continuously learning from new data and refining the detection of anomalous patterns. This integration allows for a more responsive and adaptive approach to deception, improving the ability to detect and mitigate sophisticated attacks.

Furthermore, the deployment of cloud-based deception strategies benefits from the ability to leverage threat intelligence. Integrating threat intelligence feeds into the deceptive environment can enhance the relevance and effectiveness of the decoys and honeypots deployed. By staying informed about emerging threats and attacker tactics, organizations can adjust their deceptive measures to address the latest techniques and methodologies used by adversaries. This proactive approach ensures that deceptive elements remain effective in the face of evolving threat landscapes.

In conclusion, the implementation of deception in cloud environments presents both challenges and opportunities that require a nuanced and strategic approach. By leveraging the dynamic nature of cloud computing, employing advanced technologies such as serverless computing and containerization, and incorporating behavioral analytics and threat intelligence, organizations can create highly effective deceptive measures that enhance their overall security posture. Effective management of deceptive assets, adherence to compliance requirements, and a focus on isolation and encryption are essential to ensuring the success of these strategies in a cloud context. Through careful planning and execution, deception can be a powerful tool in safeguarding against sophisticated cyber threats and enhancing an organization's ability to detect and respond to malicious activities.

CHAPTER 9:

The implementation of deceptive techniques in cybersecurity, while offering significant advantages in detecting and mitigating threats, introduces a complex interplay of legal and ethical considerations that must be navigated with care. One fundamental legal issue concerns privacy rights and the regulation of data. The nature of deception in cybersecurity often involves creating environments or scenarios that mimic real systems, which can necessitate the collection and analysis of data from users, including potentially sensitive information. This raises critical questions about how such data is handled in accordance with privacy laws and regulations.

In many jurisdictions, privacy laws are designed to protect individuals from unwarranted intrusion and misuse of their personal information. Regulations such as the General Data Protection Regulation (GDPR) in Europe and the California Consumer Privacy Act (CCPA) in the United States establish stringent requirements on how personal data must be managed, including its collection, storage, and processing. Organizations deploying deceptive techniques must ensure that their practices align with these regulations, avoiding actions that could be interpreted as unauthorized access to or misuse of personal data. This might involve implementing strict data handling protocols, ensuring that data collected during deceptive operations is anonymized or aggregated to prevent the identification of individuals, and establishing clear procedures for data access and management.

Moreover, the potential for unauthorized data access or

system interference during deceptive operations represents another significant legal concern. Deceptive environments, such as honeypots or simulated systems, must be meticulously designed and isolated from actual operational systems to prevent unintended exposure of sensitive information. Failure to secure these deceptive assets adequately could result in unauthorized access by attackers or even affect legitimate users. To mitigate these risks, organizations should implement robust isolation measures and regularly audit their deceptive environments to ensure they do not inadvertently compromise the security of their actual systems.

Ethically, the deployment of deception in cybersecurity presents its own set of challenges. The potential for misuse of deceptive techniques is a primary ethical concern. For instance, if deceptive practices are not carefully managed, they could lead to scenarios where legitimate users are incorrectly targeted or where deceptive environments are exploited for malicious purposes. It is crucial to establish clear guidelines and oversight mechanisms to ensure that deceptive techniques are used responsibly and do not result in harm to individuals or organizations. This includes designing deceptive systems to prevent misuse and ensuring that they do not inadvertently create vulnerabilities or facilitate further attacks.

Transparency is a cornerstone of ethical practice in cybersecurity deception. It involves openly communicating with stakeholders, including employees, partners, and, where appropriate, the public, about the use of deceptive techniques. Transparency helps build trust and ensures that stakeholders are informed about the potential risks and implications associated with these practices. For instance, organizations might need to inform employees about the existence of deceptive environments and their purpose, as well as establish clear protocols for how such environments are managed and monitored.

Accountability is equally important in the ethical management of deception techniques. Organizations should implement policies and procedures to hold individuals and teams responsible for the ethical use of deceptive practices. This includes setting up mechanisms for monitoring and reporting any misuse or unintended consequences of deceptive techniques. Establishing a clear chain of responsibility and ensuring that there are consequences for unethical behavior can help maintain the integrity of deceptive practices and prevent abuse.

Additionally, the ethical implications of deception extend to its impact on organizational culture and employee trust. Employees who are not aware of or do not fully understand the use of deceptive techniques may feel uneasy or distrustful of security measures. To address this, organizations should foster an open and supportive environment where employees are educated about the rationale behind deception techniques and their ethical implications. Providing training and resources to help employees navigate these practices can enhance their understanding and support for security measures.

Finally, organizations must consider the broader societal impact of their deceptive practices. The use of deception in cybersecurity can influence public perception of security practices and privacy. Ensuring that deceptive techniques are aligned with societal values and respect individual rights is essential for maintaining public trust and support. Organizations should engage with legal and ethical experts to evaluate the potential societal implications of their deceptive practices and to ensure that they adhere to best practices.

In summary, the integration of deception techniques in cybersecurity involves navigating a complex landscape of legal and ethical considerations. Addressing privacy concerns, preventing unauthorized access, and managing potential misuse are crucial for ensuring that deceptive practices are conducted responsibly. Transparency, accountability, and the consideration of broader societal impacts are key to maintaining trust and compliance. By adhering to these principles, organizations can effectively leverage deception techniques while upholding legal and ethical standards.

The implementation of deceptive techniques in cybersecurity necessitates a nuanced understanding of the legal and ethical landscape to ensure that these strategies do not inadvertently cross boundaries or infringe on rights. As we navigate this complex terrain, the principles of legality and ethics become intertwined, requiring a careful balancing act.

The use of deception, such as deploying honeypots or creating fake vulnerabilities, inherently involves the manipulation of information and environments to mislead potential attackers. This practice, while effective in many contexts, raises significant legal questions, particularly regarding privacy. The collection of data from deceptive operations must be handled in compliance with relevant data protection regulations. For instance, GDPR mandates that any data collected must be done so with explicit consent, and data subjects must be informed of how their information will be used. Even when data is collected as part of a deception strategy, it is essential to ensure that individuals' rights are not violated. This often means implementing stringent data anonymization techniques and ensuring that the data collected cannot be traced back to any individual.

Additionally, the concept of unauthorized access is a critical legal consideration. The boundaries between what constitutes authorized and unauthorized access can become blurred in deceptive scenarios. For instance, if an attacker gains access to a honeypot, the data they interact with is intentionally designed to simulate a real system, yet it may still fall under legal scrutiny if it involves sensitive or regulated data. To mitigate this risk, it is crucial to have clear policies and procedures in place that define the scope of access and interaction within deceptive environments. This includes clearly marking deceptive systems as such and ensuring they are isolated from operational systems to avoid any unintentional overlap.

On the ethical front, the potential for misuse of deceptive techniques is a significant concern. The line between using deception as a defensive measure and employing it in a manner that could be perceived as manipulative or deceptive toward legitimate users can be thin. For example, deceptive tactics should not be used in ways that could unfairly impact users or lead to unintended consequences, such as exposing them to unnecessary risks or misleading them about the security of their own data. Ethical considerations require that deceptive practices be employed with the intent of enhancing security without compromising the trust and safety of users.

Transparency and accountability play pivotal roles in addressing these ethical concerns. Transparency involves clearly communicating the presence and purpose of deceptive techniques to stakeholders, including employees, partners, and customers. This communication helps build trust and ensures that all parties are aware of the security measures in place. It is also important for organizations to have policies that govern the use of deceptive practices and to provide training to staff to ensure they understand both the legal and ethical implications of their actions.

Accountability is another cornerstone of ethical practice in cybersecurity deception. Organizations must establish clear guidelines and oversight mechanisms to monitor the implementation of deceptive techniques and to address any misuse or unintended consequences that may arise. This involves setting up internal reviews and audits to ensure that deceptive practices are used responsibly and that any issues are addressed promptly. Additionally, there should be mechanisms for reporting and addressing any ethical concerns or violations related to deceptive practices.

Furthermore, the integration of deception into cybersecurity strategies must be aligned with broader organizational values and societal expectations. This means that organizations should consider the potential societal impacts of their deceptive practices and ensure that they align with public expectations regarding privacy and security. Engaging with legal and ethical experts can help organizations navigate these complexities and ensure that their practices are in line with societal norms and expectations.

In conclusion, the deployment of deception techniques in cybersecurity involves navigating a complex landscape of legal and ethical considerations. Organizations must carefully balance the effectiveness of these techniques with the need to comply with privacy regulations and prevent unauthorized access. Ethical considerations, including the potential for misuse and the importance of transparency and accountability, must be addressed to ensure that deceptive practices are conducted responsibly. By adhering to these principles, organizations can leverage deception techniques effectively while maintaining legal and ethical integrity.

CHAPTER 10:

To further refine the assessment of deception strategies, it is crucial to delve into the nuanced aspects of measurement beyond the basic performance indicators. Evaluating the impact of deception involves examining how these strategies influence the behavior of attackers and the broader implications for security operations.

A significant component of this evaluation is understanding how deception affects attacker behavior. Effective deception should not only attract and engage adversaries but also influence their decision-making processes. This can be measured by analyzing the types of attacks conducted, the methods employed by attackers, and their persistence in attempting to compromise the system. For instance, if deceptive assets successfully mislead attackers into pursuing less critical or false targets, this can indicate that the deception strategy is working as intended. Analyzing attack patterns and success rates before and after the deployment of deception can provide insights into its effectiveness. If the frequency of successful breaches decreases, it suggests that the deceptive measures are successfully diverting or confusing attackers.

Another key aspect to consider is the integration of deception data with other security measures. Deception strategies should complement and enhance existing security tools rather than operate in isolation. Evaluating how well deception data integrates with threat intelligence platforms, incident response processes, and overall security operations can provide insights into its effectiveness. For example, if deception data enhances the accuracy of threat detection and enables more rapid incident response, it signifies that the deception strategies are contributing positively to the security framework. This integration can be measured by assessing improvements in response times, reduction in false positives, and increased accuracy of threat assessments.

The effectiveness of deception can also be gauged by its impact on organizational resilience. A robust deception strategy should contribute to the organization's ability to withstand and recover from attacks. This involves evaluating the organization's incident recovery times, the effectiveness of post-attack analyses, and the overall resilience of systems and processes. If deception strategies lead to a quicker identification of breaches and a more effective response, it demonstrates an enhancement in organizational resilience. Additionally, examining how deception influences the organization's preparedness and adaptation to emerging threats can offer valuable insights into its effectiveness.

Furthermore, the analysis of cost-effectiveness plays a critical role in evaluating deception strategies. Implementing and maintaining deception measures involves costs related to technology, resources, and personnel. It is important to assess whether the benefits gained from these strategies outweigh the costs incurred. This involves a cost-benefit analysis where the resources allocated to deception are compared against the improvements in security posture, threat detection, and overall risk reduction. Effective deception strategies should provide a measurable return on investment by reducing the frequency and impact of successful attacks, thereby justifying the costs involved.

The feedback loop from incident response teams and security analysts is another crucial element in assessing the effectiveness of deception. These stakeholders provide practical insights into how well deception strategies are integrated into daily operations and their impact on security processes. Gathering feedback on the usability, relevance, and effectiveness of deception data helps in refining and optimizing these strategies. If feedback indicates that deception data is actionable and improves decision-making, it validates the effectiveness of the approach. Conversely, if there are challenges or limitations identified, it provides an opportunity to address and enhance the deception techniques.

Finally, it is important to consider the dynamic nature of the threat landscape and its impact on deception effectiveness. As cyber threats evolve, so must deception strategies. Regularly reviewing and adapting deception techniques based on emerging threats and changes in attacker behavior is essential for maintaining effectiveness. This involves ongoing assessment and adjustment to ensure that deception strategies remain relevant and capable of countering new and sophisticated attack methods.

In conclusion, measuring the effectiveness of deception in cybersecurity requires a comprehensive approach that goes beyond basic performance indicators. By analyzing the impact on attacker behavior, integration with other security measures, organizational resilience, cost-effectiveness, and stakeholder feedback, organizations can gain a deeper understanding of how well their deception strategies are functioning. Continuous refinement and adaptation based on these evaluations ensure that deception techniques remain a vital component of a robust cybersecurity defense.

Evaluating the effectiveness of deception strategies involves more than tracking standard metrics; it requires a nuanced approach that takes into account the intricate ways in which deception influences the security environment. One significant factor to consider is how well deception aligns with organizational goals and risk management strategies. The effectiveness of a deception strategy should be measured not only by immediate outcomes but also by its ability to contribute to long-term security objectives. For instance, deception should be integrated into the broader security architecture in a way that complements and enhances existing defenses, rather than creating redundant or conflicting layers of protection. This alignment can be assessed through a strategic review of how deception integrates with other security measures, such as intrusion detection systems, firewalls, and threat intelligence platforms.

Additionally, measuring the effectiveness of deception involves analyzing how deception strategies impact the overall security posture. This includes evaluating how well deception contributes to reducing the attack surface, improving incident response times, and enhancing the organization's ability to recover from attacks. Effective deception should lead to a measurable decrease in successful attacks, an increase in early threat detection, and a reduction in the impact of breaches. These outcomes can be assessed through various methods, including tracking metrics related to attack frequency, incident response times, and recovery times.

The role of deception in shaping attacker behavior is another critical aspect of evaluation. Effective deception should influence attackers' tactics, techniques, and procedures (TTPs). By analyzing how attackers interact with deceptive elements, organizations can gain insights into the effectiveness of their strategies. For example, if attackers consistently engage with deceptive assets or are redirected away from critical systems, it indicates that the deception strategy is successfully altering their behavior. This impact can be measured by examining the changes in attack patterns and the frequency with which deceptive elements are targeted.

Moreover, the effectiveness of deception can be evaluated through the quality of threat intelligence it generates. Deception strategies should contribute to the collection of actionable intelligence about attacker behaviors, techniques, and motivations. This intelligence can be assessed by analyzing the relevance and accuracy of the information obtained from deceptive elements. High-quality threat intelligence should lead to a better understanding of emerging threats and trends, allowing for more informed decision-making and proactive security measures.

In addition to these quantitative measures, the qualitative aspects of deception effectiveness are also crucial. Gathering feedback from security analysts, incident responders, and other stakeholders provides valuable insights into how well deception strategies are functioning in practice. This feedback can highlight strengths and weaknesses in the implementation of deception techniques, as well as areas for improvement. For instance, if stakeholders report that deception data is difficult to interpret or integrate into existing workflows, it indicates a need for refinement in how deception is utilized.

The process of refining and optimizing deception strategies based on evaluation results is an ongoing one. Regular reviews and updates to deception techniques ensure that they remain effective in the face of evolving threats and changing attack patterns. This iterative process involves analyzing evaluation data, identifying areas for improvement, and implementing adjustments to enhance the effectiveness of deception strategies. For example, if analysis reveals that certain deceptive assets are not effectively attracting or engaging attackers, modifications can be made to improve their visibility or relevance.

Finally, it is important to consider the ethical implications of deception in the context of effectiveness measurement. While deception strategies can provide significant benefits in terms of enhancing security, they must be implemented with consideration for legal and ethical boundaries. Ensuring that deception measures do not inadvertently impact legitimate users or violate privacy standards is essential for maintaining ethical integrity. Effective evaluation should also include assessments of how well deception aligns with legal and ethical guidelines, ensuring that security measures do not compromise organizational values or regulatory compliance.

In summary, evaluating the effectiveness of deception strategies requires a comprehensive approach that goes beyond basic metrics. By analyzing the alignment with organizational goals, impact on security posture, influence on attacker behavior, quality of threat intelligence, and feedback from stakeholders, organizations can gain a deeper understanding of how well their deception strategies are functioning. Continuous refinement based on these evaluations ensures that deception remains a dynamic and effective component of a robust cybersecurity defense.

Future Trends in Cybersecurity Deception

As we look to the horizon of cybersecurity deception, the landscape is poised to undergo significant transformations driven by technological advancements and evolving threat paradigms. Artificial intelligence (AI) and machine learning (ML) are at the forefront of these changes, promising to revolutionize the field of deception with their capabilities to enhance, automate, and refine deception strategies.

AI and ML offer profound potential in the realm of cybersecurity deception by enabling more sophisticated and adaptive deceptive tactics. These technologies can process vast amounts of data far beyond human capabilities, identifying patterns and anomalies that might otherwise go unnoticed. For example, AI algorithms can analyze network traffic and user behavior in real time to create dynamic and context-aware deceptive elements. This allows for the development of highly tailored honeypots and decoys that adapt based on the specific tactics employed by attackers. Instead of static deception mechanisms, AI-driven deception can evolve in response to the actions of intruders, making it significantly harder for attackers to recognize and avoid these traps.

Moreover, the integration of AI into cybersecurity deception can automate the deployment and management of deceptive assets. Traditional deception strategies often require manual configuration and oversight, which can be resource-intensive and prone to human error. AI-driven systems can streamline these processes by automatically generating, deploying, and adjusting deceptive elements based on continuous threat analysis. This not only enhances the efficiency of deception but also ensures that it remains aligned with the latest threat intelligence and attack trends.

The evolution of threats is another critical factor influencing the future of cybersecurity deception. As cyber adversaries become more sophisticated, so too must our deceptive techniques. Emerging threats such as advanced persistent threats (APTs) and sophisticated ransomware attacks necessitate adaptive and resilient deception strategies. Deception must evolve to address these threats, incorporating advanced techniques such as behavioral analytics and predictive modeling to anticipate and counteract new attack vectors. For instance, using predictive analytics, organizations can anticipate the likely paths of attack and deploy deceptive elements proactively to mitigate potential breaches before they occur.

In addition to technological advancements, the increasing complexity of digital environments—such as cloud computing and Internet of Things (IoT) ecosystems—introduces new challenges for deception. As these environments expand, so does the surface area for potential attacks, making it crucial to develop deception strategies that can operate effectively across diverse and dynamic infrastructures. Future deception techniques will need to address these complexities, incorporating multi-layered deception that spans across various components of the digital landscape. This includes creating deceptive elements not only within traditional IT environments but also across cloud services, IoT devices, and other emerging technologies.

Another area of focus for the future of cybersecurity deception is the ethical and legal considerations surrounding these strategies. As deception becomes more integral to cybersecurity defenses, it is essential to navigate the balance between effective security measures and ethical boundaries. The development of transparent and accountable deception practices will be crucial to maintaining trust and compliance with legal standards. Future trends will likely involve the establishment of clear guidelines and best practices for deploying deception in a manner that respects privacy and minimizes the risk of unintended consequences.

The role of human factors in cybersecurity deception will also evolve. While AI and automation will drive many advancements, human oversight remains a critical component of effective deception strategies. Security professionals will need to continuously adapt and refine their approaches, leveraging both technological innovations and human expertise to address emerging threats and challenges. Training and skill development will be essential to equip professionals with the knowledge and tools required to implement and manage advanced deception techniques effectively.

In conclusion, the future of cybersecurity deception is characterized by rapid technological advancements and evolving threat landscapes. AI and ML will play pivotal roles in enhancing and automating deception strategies, while the increasing complexity of digital environments and the need for ethical considerations will shape the direction of these techniques. As the field continues to evolve, security professionals must remain vigilant and adaptive, integrating new technologies and practices to stay ahead of increasingly sophisticated adversaries. The convergence of technology, threat intelligence, and ethical considerations will define the next era of cybersecurity deception, providing new opportunities and challenges for the field.

As cybersecurity continues to advance, the integration of artificial intelligence (AI) and machine learning (ML) into deception strategies marks a significant shift in how we approach and implement these techniques. These technologies not only enhance the capabilities of deception but also drive its evolution by enabling more sophisticated and adaptive methods. The application of AI and ML allows for real-time analysis of complex data sets, offering insights that were previously unattainable. This data-driven approach enables the creation of dynamic deceptive elements that can adapt to the tactics and strategies employed by attackers.

The utilization of AI in deception strategies facilitates the development of intelligent honeypots and decoys. Unlike traditional static honeypots, which operate on predefined rules and responses, AI-powered honeypots can learn from interactions and adjust their behavior in real-time. This adaptability makes them more effective at misleading and trapping sophisticated attackers. By analyzing patterns in attack behavior, AI can refine and modify deceptive tactics, creating a more realistic and challenging environment for adversaries.

Machine learning algorithms further enhance deception by providing predictive capabilities. These algorithms can analyze historical attack data to forecast potential future threats and attack vectors. This forward-looking approach allows organizations to proactively deploy deceptive assets that anticipate and mitigate emerging threats before they fully materialize. For example, predictive models can suggest where attackers are most likely to strike next, enabling the strategic placement of decoys and traps in those high-risk areas.

The increasing sophistication of cyber threats necessitates a corresponding evolution in deception strategies. Advanced persistent threats (APTs) and zero-day vulnerabilities represent significant challenges, requiring more nuanced and adaptive deception techniques. The integration of AI and ML into deception strategies addresses these challenges by providing a more agile and responsive defense mechanism. AI-driven deception can simulate complex attack scenarios, allowing organizations to test and refine their response strategies in a controlled environment. This iterative process enhances the overall effectiveness of security measures and ensures that deception techniques remain relevant and impactful against evolving threats.

The rise of cloud computing and the proliferation of Internet of Things (IoT) devices introduce new dimensions to cybersecurity deception. Cloud environments present unique challenges due to their dynamic and distributed nature. Deception strategies must be adapted to address the complexities of multi-tenant environments and virtualized infrastructures. AI and ML can play a crucial role in this adaptation by managing and orchestrating deceptive elements across diverse cloud environments. These technologies can ensure that deceptive assets are appropriately distributed and configured, maintaining their effectiveness in a rapidly changing cloud landscape.

Similarly, the integration of IoT devices into deception strategies requires innovative approaches to manage and deploy deceptive elements across a vast array of interconnected devices. AI and ML can assist in identifying and simulating the behavior of various IoT devices, creating realistic decoys that mimic legitimate network traffic and device interactions. This level of granularity and realism is essential for effectively deceiving attackers who target IoT systems and networks.

Ethical considerations and legal implications also play a critical role in shaping the future of cybersecurity deception. As deception techniques become more advanced and pervasive, it is essential to address concerns related to privacy, data protection, and potential misuse. The use of AI and ML in deception raises questions about the extent to which automated systems can ethically engage in deceptive practices. Ensuring transparency and accountability in the deployment of these technologies is crucial for maintaining trust and compliance with legal and ethical standards.

The development of industry-wide best practices and guidelines will be necessary to navigate these ethical challenges. Establishing clear frameworks for the responsible use of AI and ML in deception will help mitigate potential risks and ensure that these technologies are used in a manner that aligns with legal and ethical principles. Ongoing dialogue among security professionals, policymakers, and legal experts will be essential for shaping the future direction of cybersecurity deception and addressing emerging ethical considerations.

In summary, the future of cybersecurity deception is deeply intertwined with advancements in AI and ML, which are poised to revolutionize the field by enabling more sophisticated and adaptive strategies. The integration of these technologies enhances the effectiveness of deception by providing real-time analysis, predictive capabilities, and dynamic adaptability. As cyber threats continue to evolve, the need for innovative and responsive deception techniques becomes increasingly critical. At the same time, addressing ethical and legal considerations will be essential for ensuring that these advancements are implemented responsibly and in compliance with established standards. The intersection of technology, threat evolution, and ethical considerations will define the trajectory of cybersecurity deception, shaping its role in the ongoing battle against cyber threats.

The future of cybersecurity deception will be significantly influenced by the evolution of network infrastructure and the increasing complexity of digital environments. As organizations continue to migrate to more intricate network setups, including hybrid and multi-cloud environments, the role of deception strategies must evolve to address these new challenges. The ability to effectively deploy and manage deception across diverse and fragmented networks will become a crucial factor in enhancing security posture.

Hybrid cloud environments, which combine on-premises infrastructure with cloud-based resources, introduce unique challenges for implementing deception. These environments require deception techniques that can seamlessly integrate with both traditional and cloud-based components. The complexity of these environments necessitates advanced orchestration capabilities, where AI and ML can play a pivotal role. These technologies can provide the necessary intelligence to dynamically adjust deceptive measures based on the specific characteristics of each environment, ensuring that deceptive tactics remain effective across all components of the network.

Multi-cloud deployments, where organizations use services from multiple cloud providers, further complicate the landscape. Each cloud provider has its own infrastructure and security model, which can create inconsistencies and gaps that attackers may exploit. To counter these threats, deception strategies must be adaptable and capable of working across various cloud platforms. AI and ML can aid in this adaptation by analyzing data from multiple sources and coordinating deceptive activities to cover potential vulnerabilities across different cloud environments. This level of integration is essential for maintaining a cohesive and robust defense against sophisticated cyber threats.

The growing prevalence of Internet of Things (IoT) devices adds another layer of complexity to the future of deception. IoT devices often have limited security capabilities and can serve as entry points for attackers. Deception strategies must account for the unique characteristics and behaviors of these devices. By leveraging AI and ML, organizations can create realistic simulations of IoT device interactions, making it more challenging for attackers to distinguish between legitimate and deceptive elements. Furthermore, the ability to analyze and respond to data generated by IoT devices in real-time enhances the effectiveness of deception by providing timely insights into potential threats and anomalies.

The integration of blockchain technology also presents opportunities for advancing deception strategies. Blockchain's decentralized nature and immutability can be leveraged to enhance the integrity and traceability of deceptive operations. For example, blockchain can be used to securely log and verify interactions with deceptive elements, ensuring that any manipulation or tampering is detected and recorded. This additional layer of security can enhance the credibility of deceptive measures and provide valuable evidence for forensic investigations.

Ethical considerations will continue to be a critical aspect of the evolving landscape of cybersecurity deception. As deception techniques become more advanced, ensuring that they are used responsibly and ethically will be paramount. The deployment of sophisticated deceptive technologies must be accompanied by clear guidelines and oversight to prevent misuse and protect privacy. Developing and adhering to ethical standards will help maintain trust among stakeholders and ensure that deception remains a valuable tool in the cybersecurity arsenal without crossing ethical boundaries.

Moreover, the collaboration between industry, academia, and regulatory bodies will play a crucial role in shaping the future of deception in cybersecurity. Research and development efforts must focus on exploring new deception techniques, evaluating their effectiveness, and addressing emerging challenges. Collaborative initiatives can drive innovation and facilitate the sharing of best practices and lessons learned. This collective effort will help advance the field and ensure that deception strategies remain effective in addressing the evolving threat landscape.

In conclusion, the future of cybersecurity deception will be shaped by advancements in technology, including AI, ML, blockchain, and the increasing complexity of network environments. The ability to effectively integrate deception across hybrid and multi-cloud environments, manage IoT devices, and leverage emerging technologies will be crucial for maintaining a robust security posture. At the same time, ethical considerations and collaborative efforts will guide the responsible use of deception techniques and drive innovation in the field. As the cybersecurity landscape continues to evolve, deception will remain a dynamic and essential component of a comprehensive security strategy, adapting to new challenges and opportunities as they arise.

Implementing Deception in Cloud Environments

Adapting deception techniques for cloud environments necessitates a nuanced understanding of both cloud infrastructure and the specific challenges it presents. Cloud computing introduces a layer of complexity that differs significantly from traditional on-premises setups, impacting how deceptive measures are implemented and managed. In exploring these adaptations, I delve into the unique characteristics of cloud environments, including the shared responsibility model, the elasticity of resources, and the diversity of cloud services.

One of the foremost challenges in deploying deception in cloud environments is the shared responsibility model, which delineates the security responsibilities between the cloud provider and the customer. In this model, while the cloud provider is responsible for securing the underlying infrastructure, the customer is responsible for the security of the applications and data they deploy. This division requires a tailored approach to deception, where deceptive assets must be designed and managed with an understanding of the boundaries of responsibility.

Deploying virtual honeypots in cloud environments offers a method for detecting and analyzing attacks within a controlled setting. Unlike traditional honeypots, which are often physically isolated, cloud-based honeypots must be capable of scaling dynamically with the cloud infrastructure. Virtual honeypots can be instantiated as needed, allowing them to adapt to the fluctuating demands of cloud resources. This flexibility is crucial for maintaining the effectiveness of deception, as it ensures that honeypots can be deployed in response to emerging threats without overburdening the cloud infrastructure.

Cloud-based decoys and traps also need to be designed with the inherent scalability and multi-tenancy of cloud environments in mind. Decoys can be integrated into various cloud services, including storage and computing resources, to create realistic environments that lure attackers. For instance, a decoy file storage system might contain fake but plausible data, while a decoy application server could simulate a vulnerable service. These decoys must be meticulously crafted to blend with genuine resources to avoid detection and ensure that attackers engage with them.

The integration of deception with cloud security practices involves a strategic approach to monitoring and incident response. Cloud environments provide extensive logging and monitoring capabilities, which can be leveraged to enhance the effectiveness of deceptive measures. By integrating deceptive elements with cloud-native monitoring tools, organizations can track interactions with deceptive assets in real-time and correlate these interactions with other security events. This integration enables a more comprehensive view of potential threats and facilitates a quicker response to suspicious activities.

Effective incident response in cloud environments requires that deceptive measures are well-coordinated with the organization's overall security strategy. Cloud platforms offer various incident response tools and services that can be used in conjunction with deception techniques. For example, automated response actions can be configured to react to alerts generated by deceptive assets, such as isolating affected resources or triggering forensic investigations. This automated approach enhances the agility of incident response and ensures that deceptive measures are seamlessly integrated into the broader security framework.

Furthermore, managing deceptive assets in a multi-tenant cloud environment presents additional considerations. In such environments, multiple customers share the same cloud infrastructure, which can complicate the deployment and management of deceptive measures. To address these challenges, organizations must ensure that deceptive assets are isolated and do not inadvertently affect other tenants. Techniques such as network segmentation and strict access controls can help maintain the integrity of deceptive measures and prevent cross-tenant contamination.

One practical strategy for implementing deception in cloud environments is to leverage containerization and microservices architecture. Containers allow for the rapid deployment of isolated deceptive environments that can mimic real applications or services. This approach not only simplifies the management of deceptive assets but also provides a high degree of flexibility and scalability. Microservices, on the other hand, enable the creation of modular and dynamically configurable deceptive components that can be orchestrated to simulate complex attack scenarios.

In summary, adapting deception techniques for cloud environments involves addressing the unique characteristics and challenges of cloud-based infrastructures. By deploying virtual honeypots, decoys, and traps that are designed to scale and integrate with cloud security practices, organizations can effectively detect and respond to attacks. The strategic integration of deception with cloud monitoring and incident response tools further enhances the effectiveness of these measures. As cloud environments continue to evolve, the adaptation of deception techniques will play a crucial role in maintaining robust security defenses.

Implementing deception in cloud environments requires a careful consideration of both the inherent benefits and limitations presented by cloud technologies. The dynamic nature of cloud environments necessitates a flexible and scalable approach to deploying deception measures. To be effective, these measures must align with the operational and security characteristics of cloud infrastructures.

One key consideration in deploying virtual honeypots in cloud environments is their ability to adapt to the highly dynamic nature of cloud resources. Unlike traditional physical honeypots, which are fixed in location, cloud-based honeypots must be able to scale up or down in response to changes in demand. This scalability ensures that the honeypots remain effective in detecting and engaging with attackers, regardless of the current load on the cloud infrastructure. Additionally, the use of cloud-native technologies such as containerization can enhance the flexibility and deployability of these honeypots. Containers allow for the rapid provisioning of isolated environments that can simulate various attack surfaces and vulnerabilities, thus providing a more realistic and engaging target for attackers.

When deploying decoys and traps in a cloud environment, it is essential to consider the multi-tenancy of cloud platforms. In a shared cloud infrastructure, multiple customers or tenants may operate within the same physical hardware, leading to potential issues with isolation and interference. Effective implementation of decoys and traps requires careful design to ensure that these deceptive assets do not inadvertently impact or expose other tenants' data or operations. Techniques such as virtual network segmentation, strict access controls, and monitoring can help mitigate these risks and maintain the integrity of the deceptive measures.

Furthermore, the integration of deception techniques with cloud security practices must address the challenges posed by the cloud's elastic nature. Cloud environments can automatically adjust resource allocation based on demand, which can affect the availability and performance of deceptive assets. To ensure that deception measures remain effective, they should be designed to integrate seamlessly with cloud-based security monitoring and incident response tools. This integration allows for real-time tracking of interactions with deceptive assets and facilitates a coordinated response to potential threats.

Monitoring and incident response are critical components of effective deception strategies in cloud environments. Cloud platforms offer a range of monitoring tools and services that can be leveraged to enhance the effectiveness of deceptive measures. By integrating deception with cloud-native monitoring solutions, organizations can gain deeper visibility into potential threats and their interactions with deceptive assets. This visibility enables more accurate detection of malicious activities and provides valuable insights into attack patterns and methods.

One practical approach to integrating deception with cloud-based monitoring is to utilize advanced analytics and machine learning algorithms. These technologies can analyze large volumes of data generated by deceptive assets and identify patterns indicative of malicious behavior. For example, machine learning models can detect anomalies in the interactions with decoys and traps, providing early warning signs of potential attacks. The ability to automate the analysis and response processes through machine learning can significantly enhance the agility and effectiveness of deception strategies.

Incident response in cloud environments also benefits from automation and orchestration capabilities. Cloud platforms often provide tools for automating response actions based on predefined criteria, such as isolating compromised resources or initiating forensic investigations. By integrating deceptive measures with these automated response mechanisms, organizations can quickly address threats and minimize the impact of attacks. This approach ensures that deceptive assets are effectively utilized as part of a broader security strategy, providing a comprehensive defense against sophisticated threats.

The deployment of deceptive assets in cloud environments also requires ongoing management and maintenance to ensure their continued effectiveness. Regular updates and adjustments to the deceptive assets are necessary to keep pace with evolving threats and changes in the cloud environment. This includes updating the configurations of honeypots, decoys, and traps to reflect new attack vectors and vulnerabilities. Additionally, continuous monitoring and analysis of interactions with deceptive assets can provide valuable feedback for refining and optimizing the deception strategies.

In conclusion, implementing deception in cloud environments involves addressing the unique challenges and opportunities presented by cloud technologies. By leveraging cloud-native capabilities and integrating deception with monitoring and incident response practices, organizations can enhance their security posture and effectively detect and mitigate attacks. The use of advanced technologies such as containerization, machine learning, and automation further strengthens the effectiveness of deception measures, providing a robust defense against emerging threats in cloud environments.

The successful implementation of deception in cloud environments involves a nuanced approach that addresses both technological and strategic considerations. One of the primary challenges in this domain is ensuring that deceptive measures align with the cloud's inherent characteristics, such as elasticity, multi-tenancy, and distributed nature. To effectively deploy deception strategies, it is crucial to understand how these characteristics impact the deployment and management of deceptive assets.

The dynamic and scalable nature of cloud environments means that deceptive assets must be adaptable to changing conditions. Cloud platforms are designed to scale resources up or down based on demand, which can affect the performance and availability of deceptive elements like honeypots, decoys, and traps. To maintain their effectiveness, these deceptive measures need to be designed with elasticity in mind. This requires the use of automated provisioning and scaling tools to ensure that deceptive assets can grow or shrink in response to traffic patterns and threat activities.

Virtual honeypots, for instance, must be capable of dynamic allocation and deallocation within the cloud. This means that rather than relying on static configurations, virtual honeypots should be integrated with cloud orchestration tools that can automatically adjust their deployment based on real-time data. Such tools can spin up new honeypots or scale existing ones in response to detected threats, ensuring that deceptive measures remain relevant and effective.

Another significant consideration is the management of deceptive assets within multi-tenant cloud environments. Multi-tenancy introduces complexities related to isolation and security. Deceptive assets must be carefully designed to avoid interference with other tenants' data or resources. This involves employing advanced network segmentation and access control mechanisms to ensure that deceptive elements are contained and do not inadvertently affect other users or expose sensitive data. Proper configuration of virtual private clouds (VPCs) and network access control lists (ACLs) can help achieve this isolation.

When integrating deception techniques with cloud security practices, it is essential to consider how deception can be combined with existing security controls to enhance overall effectiveness. For example, deception measures can be integrated with cloud-native security monitoring tools to provide a more comprehensive view of the threat landscape. This integration allows for the real-time monitoring of interactions with deceptive assets, enabling quicker detection of potential threats and more accurate analysis of attack patterns.

Incident response strategies in cloud environments benefit significantly from the integration of deception techniques. Cloud platforms often provide automation and orchestration capabilities that can enhance incident response efforts. By linking deceptive measures with automated response workflows, organizations can quickly isolate and address threats. For instance, if a decoy is triggered, an automated response could involve isolating the affected resources, alerting security teams, and initiating a forensic investigation. This automation ensures that deceptive assets are not only detected but also effectively leveraged in real-time threat scenarios.

The integration of advanced analytics and machine learning further enhances the effectiveness of deception strategies in cloud environments. Machine learning algorithms can analyze large volumes of data generated by deceptive assets, identifying patterns and anomalies that might indicate malicious activity. This capability allows for the proactive detection of threats and provides valuable insights into the tactics, techniques, and procedures used by attackers. Incorporating these analytics into cloud security operations enables more informed decision-making and improves the precision of response actions.

Regular updates and maintenance of deceptive assets are crucial for maintaining their relevance and effectiveness. As cloud environments evolve and new threats emerge, deceptive measures must be adapted to address changing conditions. This includes updating the configurations of honeypots, decoys, and traps to reflect new attack vectors and vulnerabilities. Continuous monitoring and feedback from interactions with deceptive assets can guide these updates, ensuring that deception strategies remain aligned with the current threat landscape.

The effectiveness of deception in cloud environments also depends on the ability to assess and refine strategies based on performance metrics. Organizations should establish metrics to evaluate the success of deceptive measures, such as the frequency of interactions with decoys, the types of attacks detected, and the overall impact on security posture. Analyzing these metrics helps in refining deception techniques, optimizing their deployment, and ensuring that they provide maximum value in defending against threats.

In summary, implementing deception in cloud environments requires a strategic approach that considers the unique characteristics of cloud technologies and integrates deception with existing security practices. By leveraging automation, advanced analytics, and continuous monitoring, organizations can effectively deploy and manage deceptive assets in dynamic and multi-tenant cloud environments. This approach enhances the ability to detect and respond to threats, providing a robust defense mechanism against sophisticated cyber attacks.

CHAPTER 11:

In addressing the application of cybersecurity deception within industrial control systems (ICS), it is crucial to delve into the specific nature of threats these environments face and how tailored deception techniques can effectively mitigate these risks. Industrial control systems, integral to managing critical infrastructure such as power grids, water treatment facilities, and manufacturing plants, face unique challenges due to their operational requirements and the potential impact of disruptions.

The industrial control environment operates under a paradigm where the integrity and availability of physical processes are paramount. Unlike traditional IT systems, ICS environments require uninterrupted operation to ensure safety and efficiency. This makes them particularly vulnerable to attacks that aim to disrupt processes or cause physical damage. Threat actors targeting ICS can range from cybercriminals seeking financial gain to state-sponsored groups aiming to cause widespread disruption or espionage. These adversaries often exploit vulnerabilities in both hardware and software, necessitating advanced and adaptive defense strategies.

Deception techniques in ICS must therefore be meticulously crafted to reflect the specific characteristics and operational aspects of these systems. Implementing honeypots and decoys requires a nuanced approach to ensure that these deceptive tools effectively mimic real operational components without disrupting actual processes. For instance, honeypots designed for ICS must replicate the behavior of industrial devices such as programmable logic controllers (PLCs), remote terminal units (RTUs), and SCADA systems with high fidelity. These honeypots can be configured to simulate various operational states and responses, creating a realistic environment that can lure attackers and provide insights into their methods and objectives.

One key aspect of deploying honeypots in ICS environments involves ensuring that these deceptive elements are sufficiently isolated from operational systems to prevent accidental interference. Network segmentation and rigorous access controls are essential to create a boundary between deceptive and genuine systems. This isolation not only safeguards the integrity of real ICS components but also ensures that interactions with honeypots do not lead to false positives or unintended disruptions. The honeypots should be designed to record all interactions meticulously, providing valuable data on attack vectors, techniques, and tools used by adversaries.

In addition to honeypots, the deployment of decoys within ICS can significantly enhance the ability to detect and analyze cyber threats. Decoys are designed to replicate the appearance and functionality of critical control components and processes. For example, a decoy could mimic the behavior of a critical data acquisition point or a crucial control command, thereby creating a misleading environment that attracts attackers. The interactions with these decoys can reveal attack patterns and tactics, contributing to a deeper understanding of potential threats.

The integration of deception techniques with existing security practices is another critical consideration. Effective monitoring and incident response capabilities must be in place to complement deceptive measures. Continuous monitoring tools can be employed to track interactions with deceptive assets, providing real-time visibility into potential attacks. This data can be analyzed to identify trends, detect anomalies, and generate actionable intelligence. By correlating information from honeypots and decoys with other security data, such as network traffic logs and system alerts, security teams can gain a comprehensive view of the threat landscape and enhance their response strategies.

The implementation of deception in ICS also necessitates ongoing evaluation and adaptation. The threat landscape in industrial environments is continually evolving, with new vulnerabilities and attack methods emerging regularly. To maintain the effectiveness of deception techniques, it is essential to regularly update honeypots and decoys to reflect changes in the operational environment and threat landscape. Periodic assessments and testing can help identify weaknesses and ensure that deceptive elements remain relevant and effective.

Collaboration and coordination among various stakeholders are crucial for the successful implementation of deception in ICS. IT and operational technology (OT) teams must work together to ensure that deceptive measures are aligned with the overall security strategy and operational requirements. Effective communication between these teams can facilitate the integration of deception with other security measures and ensure that all personnel are aware of their roles and responsibilities in managing deceptive elements. Training and awareness programs can further support this collaboration by providing insights into the role of deception in the security posture and enhancing the ability to respond to potential incidents.

In summary, the application of cybersecurity deception within industrial control systems involves a sophisticated approach tailored to the unique characteristics and threats faced by these environments. By deploying well-designed honeypots and decoys, integrating deception with existing security practices, and maintaining ongoing evaluation and adaptation, organizations can enhance their ability to detect and respond to sophisticated cyber threats. The successful implementation of these techniques requires careful planning, coordination, and continuous improvement to safeguard the integrity and resilience of critical infrastructure.

In implementing deception within industrial control systems (ICS), it is imperative to consider the operational constraints and safety concerns unique to these environments. Industrial control systems, integral to sectors such as energy, water, and manufacturing, manage and monitor critical processes that, if disrupted, could lead to severe consequences. Therefore, the application of deception techniques must be conducted with a focus on minimizing risk while maximizing the efficacy of threat detection and mitigation.

One of the core challenges in deploying deception within ICS is ensuring that these measures do not inadvertently impact operational systems. Industrial environments often operate under stringent reliability and safety standards, and any interference could have disastrous effects. Consequently, deception techniques must be carefully designed and integrated to avoid introducing vulnerabilities or causing disruptions. This involves creating a clear demarcation between operational systems and deceptive elements, often through network segmentation and strict access controls. By isolating deceptive assets from real operational systems, organizations can prevent accidental interactions that might compromise the integrity of critical processes.

The deployment of honeypots in ICS environments requires a tailored approach to accurately simulate the behavior of industrial devices and processes. For instance, honeypots can be configured to mimic the operation of programmable logic controllers (PLCs), supervisory control and data acquisition (SCADA) systems, or other critical components. These honeypots should be designed to generate realistic traffic and responses to attract potential attackers. Their configuration should reflect the operational characteristics and vulnerabilities of actual ICS devices to ensure that they effectively lure and engage adversaries. This realistic simulation helps in collecting actionable intelligence about attack methods and tools, providing insights that can enhance the overall security posture.

Similarly, the implementation of decoys within ICS involves creating false representations of critical control points and processes. These decoys are designed to appear as genuine components, drawing attackers away from actual operational systems. Effective decoys should be crafted to emulate the functionality of key system elements, such as control interfaces or data acquisition points. By analyzing interactions with these decoys, security teams can gain valuable insights into attack strategies and objectives. The data gathered from decoy interactions can inform adjustments to security measures and improve response strategies.

Integrating deception with existing ICS security practices involves aligning deceptive measures with broader monitoring and incident response strategies. Continuous monitoring tools should be employed to track interactions with honeypots and decoys, providing real-time visibility into potential threats. This integration allows for a comprehensive view of the security landscape, combining data from deceptive elements with other sources of security information, such as network traffic logs and system alerts. Correlating this data can help in identifying and responding to threats more effectively.

Incident response in the context of ICS deception requires careful coordination to ensure that deceptive measures are used to support, rather than disrupt, the response process. Security teams must be prepared to analyze data from honeypots and decoys to determine the nature and scope of an attack. This involves evaluating the interactions captured by deceptive elements and correlating them with other security events. Effective incident response plans should include procedures for handling deceptive data, ensuring that it is used to enhance situational awareness and guide response efforts.

Ongoing evaluation and refinement of deception techniques are essential to maintaining their effectiveness in dynamic threat environments. The threat landscape in ICS environments is continually evolving, with new vulnerabilities and attack methods emerging regularly. To keep pace with these changes, it is important to periodically review and update honeypots and decoys. This might involve adjusting their configurations to reflect new attack techniques or incorporating new types of deceptive elements to address emerging threats. Regular testing and assessment can help identify weaknesses and ensure that deceptive measures remain relevant and effective.

Collaboration between IT and operational technology (OT) teams is critical for the successful implementation of deception in ICS. These teams must work together to ensure that deceptive measures are integrated seamlessly with existing security practices and operational requirements. Effective communication and coordination can facilitate the alignment of deception strategies with overall security objectives and ensure that all stakeholders are aware of their roles and responsibilities. Training and awareness programs can further support this collaboration by providing insights into the role of deception in ICS security and enhancing the ability to respond to potential incidents.

In conclusion, the application of cybersecurity deception within industrial control systems presents a complex but valuable approach to enhancing security. By carefully designing and implementing honeypots and decoys, integrating deception with existing security practices, and maintaining ongoing evaluation and adaptation, organizations can effectively mitigate the risks posed by sophisticated cyber threats. The successful deployment of these techniques requires a nuanced understanding of the unique challenges and constraints of ICS environments, as well as careful planning and coordination among security professionals. Through these efforts, organizations can better protect critical infrastructure and ensure the continued safety and reliability of their industrial control systems.

CHAPTER 12:

The landscape of cybersecurity deception is undergoing a profound transformation driven by technological advancements. As I delve deeper into these advanced techniques, it becomes evident that the integration of artificial intelligence and machine learning is pivotal to the evolution of effective deception strategies. These technologies are not merely enhancements but foundational elements that redefine how deception is conceived and implemented in the realm of cybersecurity.

Artificial intelligence plays a crucial role in enhancing deception strategies by enabling the creation of highly sophisticated decoys and traps. Traditional decoys, while effective, often rely on static configurations that can become predictable over time. In contrast, AI-driven decoys leverage advanced algorithms to create dynamic environments that can adapt in real time. These decoys are designed to emulate complex systems with high fidelity, making them more challenging for attackers to distinguish from genuine assets. By analyzing patterns in attack behavior, AI can continuously refine the characteristics and responses of decoys, thus increasing their efficacy.

Machine learning further augments deception techniques by providing the capability to analyze vast amounts of data and identify subtle patterns that may indicate an attack. For instance, machine learning algorithms can be used to detect anomalies in network traffic or user behavior that may not be immediately apparent through conventional monitoring methods. This capability allows for the development of adaptive honeypots that can alter their configuration and interactions based on the evolving tactics of attackers. These honeypots are not only more difficult for attackers to bypass but also more effective in gathering detailed intelligence about attack methods and objectives.

Behavioral analytics is another critical component that complements AI and machine learning in advanced deception strategies. By continuously monitoring and analyzing the behavior of users and systems, behavioral analytics can provide insights into abnormal activities that may signify an ongoing attack. This approach enables the creation of more realistic and responsive deceptive environments. For example, if an attacker starts exploiting a vulnerability in a novel way, behavioral analytics can detect this change and trigger corresponding adjustments in the deceptive measures. This ensures that the deception remains relevant and effective against new and emerging threats.

Integrating AI and machine learning into deception technology involves several key considerations to ensure effectiveness and security. The development of these technologies requires extensive training data, which must be accurate and comprehensive to produce reliable results. Collecting and analyzing data on various attack vectors, threat actor behaviors, and system responses is essential for training machine learning models that drive deception tools. Continuous data acquisition and model refinement are crucial to keep pace with evolving threats and maintain the effectiveness of deception strategies.

Securing the AI and machine learning components of deception technology is equally important. As these technologies become more integral to cybersecurity defenses, they also become potential targets for attackers. Ensuring that AI models and their underlying data are protected from unauthorized access and manipulation is essential. This involves implementing robust security measures such as encryption, access controls, and regular audits to safeguard the integrity of the deception tools.

Advanced deception technologies also benefit from a multi-layered approach that integrates various types of deception techniques across different layers of the IT infrastructure. This strategy involves deploying multiple deceptive elements, such as network-level decoys, application-level traps, and data-level honeypots. Each layer serves a specific purpose and contributes to a comprehensive deception strategy. For instance, network-level decoys can simulate network infrastructure, while application-level traps can mimic critical business applications, and data-level honeypots can create fake data stores. By engaging attackers at multiple points within the IT environment, organizations can increase the complexity of the deceptive landscape and gather more comprehensive intelligence about attack methods.

Moreover, the implementation of advanced deception techniques requires a thorough understanding of the organizational environment and its specific threat landscape. Tailoring deception strategies to the unique characteristics of the IT infrastructure, business processes, and threat vectors is crucial for achieving optimal results. This involves conducting a detailed assessment of the organization's security posture, identifying potential vulnerabilities, and designing deception measures that align with the overall security objectives.

The continuous evolution of deception technology necessitates staying abreast of emerging trends and advancements. As the field of cybersecurity deception progresses, new techniques and technologies will likely emerge, offering novel ways to enhance security. By embracing these advancements and adapting to the changing threat landscape, organizations can strengthen their defenses and better protect their critical assets from cyber adversaries.

In summary, the integration of artificial intelligence, machine learning, and behavioral analytics represents a significant leap forward in the effectiveness of deception technologies. These advanced techniques enable the creation of dynamic, adaptive, and intelligent deception strategies that can better withstand sophisticated cyber attacks. By leveraging these technologies, organizations can enhance their ability to detect, mitigate, and respond to evolving threats, thereby fortifying their overall cybersecurity posture.

As we advance further into the realm of cutting-edge deception technologies, it becomes evident that the integration of emerging trends and techniques is shaping a new era of cybersecurity defense. A particularly transformative development is the use of artificial intelligence (AI) to enhance the sophistication and effectiveness of deception mechanisms. AI-driven systems enable a more nuanced and responsive approach to deception, making it increasingly difficult for attackers to discern real from deceptive assets.

One of the most promising applications of AI in deception technology is the development of intelligent decoys. Unlike traditional decoys, which are static and predictable, AI-enhanced decoys employ machine learning algorithms to dynamically alter their behavior and appearance in real time. These decoys can simulate a wide range of activities and interactions, mimicking legitimate systems with high fidelity. By doing so, they create a more immersive and convincing environment for attackers. AI can analyze incoming traffic and attacker behavior, adjusting the decoy's responses to align with observed tactics and techniques, thereby increasing the likelihood of successful engagement and detection.

In parallel, adaptive honeypots represent another advanced technique facilitated by AI. Traditional honeypots are designed to attract and trap attackers by mimicking vulnerable systems. However, their effectiveness can be limited by their static nature. Adaptive honeypots, powered by AI, go a step further by learning from interactions and modifying their configuration based on attacker behavior. This dynamic adaptability enables the honeypots to stay relevant and effective against evolving attack strategies. For instance, if an attacker uses a novel exploit or attack vector, the honeypot can reconfigure itself to emulate vulnerabilities associated with the new technique, thereby maintaining its attractiveness and utility.

Machine learning also plays a critical role in enhancing the effectiveness of deception strategies through behavioral analytics. By analyzing patterns in network traffic, user behavior, and system interactions, machine learning models can identify anomalies and deviations from normal activity. These deviations may indicate potential attacks or suspicious behavior that warrants further investigation. Behavioral analytics can be integrated with deception technologies to create environments that not only lure attackers but also intelligently respond to their actions. For example, if an attacker begins to exploit a previously unseen vulnerability, the system can adjust its deceptive elements to simulate this new vulnerability, thus maintaining the integrity of the deception.

Furthermore, the integration of AI and machine learning with deception technologies requires a robust infrastructure to handle the increased complexity and volume of data. High-performance computing resources and advanced data processing capabilities are essential to support the real-time analysis and response demands of these technologies. The deployment of such infrastructure must be carefully planned and managed to ensure that it does not introduce new vulnerabilities or performance bottlenecks.

As we explore the integration of advanced techniques, it is also crucial to address the challenges associated with implementing and managing these technologies. One significant challenge is ensuring the accuracy and reliability of AI and machine learning models. The effectiveness of deception technologies depends on the quality of the data used to train these models. Inaccurate or incomplete data can lead to ineffective or even counterproductive deception. Therefore, continuous monitoring, evaluation, and refinement of AI and machine learning models are necessary to maintain their effectiveness and relevance.

Moreover, ethical considerations and the potential for misuse of advanced deception technologies must be carefully managed. While these technologies offer significant advantages in terms of detection and mitigation, they also raise concerns about privacy, data protection, and the potential for unintended consequences. Organizations must establish clear policies and guidelines for the use of deception technologies, ensuring that they are deployed in a manner that aligns with legal and ethical standards. Transparency and accountability in the implementation and management of these technologies are essential to address these concerns and build trust among stakeholders.

In addition to these challenges, the future of advanced deception technologies will likely be shaped by ongoing advancements in related fields. For instance, the development of quantum computing could introduce new opportunities and challenges for deception strategies. Quantum computing promises to enhance computational power, potentially enabling more sophisticated and complex deception mechanisms. Conversely, it may also pose new risks by potentially breaking existing cryptographic protections. Staying informed about these developments and their implications will be crucial for adapting and evolving deception strategies.

Overall, the integration of AI, machine learning, and behavioral analytics into deception technologies represents a significant leap forward in cybersecurity. These advanced techniques enable a more dynamic, adaptive, and effective approach to deception, enhancing the ability to detect and respond to sophisticated cyber threats. By addressing the challenges and ethical considerations associated with these technologies, organizations can leverage their capabilities to strengthen their cybersecurity defenses and better protect their critical assets. The continued evolution of deception technologies will undoubtedly play a pivotal role in shaping the future of cybersecurity and the ongoing battle against cyber adversaries.

CHAPTER 13:

The implementation of deception in cybersecurity must be carefully evaluated through the lens of legal and ethical standards. When deploying deceptive practices, such as honeypots, decoys, or traps, organizations face a complex landscape of regulations and ethical dilemmas that demand meticulous consideration.

First and foremost, the legal implications of deception involve navigating privacy laws, which vary significantly across jurisdictions. In many regions, privacy laws are designed to protect individuals' data and limit the ways in which it can be collected and used. For example, the General Data Protection Regulation (GDPR) in the European Union enforces strict guidelines on data processing and demands transparency from organizations regarding how personal data is handled. Similarly, the California Consumer Privacy Act (CCPA) provides residents of California with certain rights over their personal information. When employing deceptive techniques, it is crucial to ensure that these practices do not violate privacy regulations. This means implementing safeguards to prevent the collection of unnecessary personal data and ensuring that any data collected through deceptive methods is handled in compliance with relevant laws.

Consent is another critical area of concern when it comes to legal compliance. The concept of consent, particularly in the context of data collection, is foundational in many legal frameworks. Organizations must be transparent about their data collection practices and obtain consent where required.

However, in the realm of deception, obtaining explicit consent can be challenging. For instance, the use of deceptive honeypots or traps may involve collecting data from users without their knowledge, which raises questions about the legality and ethics of such practices. To navigate these challenges, organizations should develop clear policies regarding consent and ensure that their deception strategies are designed to comply with legal requirements. This might involve incorporating mechanisms for users to opt out of data collection or ensuring that any data collected is anonymized and aggregated to prevent the identification of individuals.

Legal boundaries also come into play when considering the scope and limitations of deception techniques. Unauthorized access to systems or data, even with the intention of detecting malicious activity, can lead to legal consequences. The deployment of deception must be confined to systems and networks that the organization has explicit permission to monitor. Engaging in activities that extend beyond authorized boundaries could be construed as illegal, resulting in potential legal liabilities. Therefore, it is imperative for organizations to clearly define the parameters within which their deception strategies operate and to ensure that they adhere to legal standards concerning authorization and access control.

Ethical considerations further complicate the deployment of deception. The impact of deceptive practices on innocent parties is a significant ethical concern. Deception strategies, by their nature, involve some level of misdirection or false information, which can potentially affect individuals who are not the intended targets. For example, a honeypot designed to attract attackers might inadvertently capture data from legitimate users who interact with the decoy. Such unintended consequences can lead to privacy infringements or operational disruptions for innocent parties. To address these ethical concerns, organizations must carefully design their deception strategies to minimize harm and ensure that any impact on users is justified by the security benefits gained. This involves implementing measures to mitigate the risk of affecting legitimate users and maintaining a balance between effective deception and ethical responsibility.

Transparency is another key ethical principle in the context of deception. While deception inherently involves concealing certain aspects of an organization's security measures, it is important to maintain transparency regarding the overall purpose and scope of these practices. Transparency with stakeholders, including employees, customers, and partners, helps to build trust and ensure that there is a clear understanding of how deception is being employed. This can involve communicating the goals of the deception strategy, the types of data being collected, and the measures taken to protect privacy. By fostering an open dialogue about the use of deception, organizations can address potential concerns and reinforce their commitment to ethical practices.

Additionally, the ethical deployment of deception requires addressing potential biases and ensuring fairness in its application. Deceptive practices should not target or discriminate against specific individuals or groups unfairly. Biases in the design or execution of deception strategies can lead to ethical issues and undermine the effectiveness of the approach. It is crucial for organizations to continuously evaluate their deception practices to ensure they align with ethical standards and do not perpetuate discrimination or unfair treatment.

Finally, staying abreast of evolving legal and ethical standards is essential for maintaining compliance and integrity in the deployment of deception. As the field of cybersecurity evolves and new regulations or ethical norms emerge, organizations must adapt their practices accordingly. Regularly reviewing and updating policies and procedures helps to ensure that deception strategies remain legally and ethically sound.

In conclusion, the legal and ethical dimensions of deploying deception in cybersecurity require careful consideration and adherence to established standards. By addressing privacy concerns, obtaining proper consent, respecting legal boundaries, and upholding ethical principles, organizations can effectively utilize deception while maintaining legal compliance and ethical integrity.

The implementation of deception in cybersecurity is not without its complexities, especially when examining the broader legal and ethical landscape. Beyond the immediate concerns of privacy, consent, and legal boundaries, several additional factors play crucial roles in shaping responsible and effective deception strategies.

One of the more intricate aspects of deploying deception is ensuring that practices align with international regulations and standards. As organizations increasingly operate in a global environment, they must navigate a patchwork of legal frameworks that govern data privacy and cybersecurity. For instance, regulations like the GDPR in the European Union and the CCPA in California set stringent requirements on how data is managed, with significant implications for deception techniques that involve data collection. The interplay between these regulations can create challenges for organizations seeking to implement deception strategies across different jurisdictions. To address this, it is imperative to adopt a multi-jurisdictional approach to compliance, involving legal counsel familiar with international regulations. This approach ensures that deception practices are not only legally compliant but also harmonized with the diverse regulatory requirements of different regions.

Another critical consideration is the role of consent in the context of organizational transparency and accountability. In addition to adhering to legal consent requirements, organizations must consider the ethical implications of obtaining consent in scenarios where deception is used. Traditional models of consent may not always align with the nature of deceptive practices, which often involve concealed or misleading elements. As a result, organizations must develop innovative approaches to consent that balance legal requirements with the ethical need for transparency. For instance, they might implement layered consent mechanisms where users are informed about the general use of data and potential deceptive practices in a manner that is clear and comprehensible.

The principle of proportionality is also essential when evaluating the ethical implications of deception. Deceptive techniques should be proportionate to the risks they aim to mitigate. This means that the extent of deception deployed should correspond to the severity of the threat and the potential impact on stakeholders. Implementing overly aggressive or intrusive deception tactics may not only breach legal boundaries but also result in ethical dilemmas, such as the unnecessary compromise of user privacy or the inadvertent disruption of legitimate activities. Organizations must continuously assess the proportionality of their deception strategies, ensuring that they are justified by the security needs and balanced against potential harms.

Furthermore, there is an increasing emphasis on the ethical responsibility of organizations to protect not just their own interests but also the broader public interest. Deception strategies must be designed with consideration for their broader societal impact, including potential effects on public trust and safety. For example, deceptive techniques that inadvertently expose sensitive information or disrupt essential services could have far-reaching consequences beyond the immediate security context. Organizations should adopt a holistic approach to evaluating the societal implications of their deception practices, engaging with stakeholders and experts to understand and mitigate potential risks.

The evolving nature of technology and cybersecurity also necessitates ongoing ethical reflection. As new technologies and methodologies emerge, they bring novel ethical and legal challenges. For instance, advancements in artificial intelligence and machine learning introduce new dimensions to deception, such as the use of sophisticated algorithms to create realistic decoys or to simulate complex attack scenarios. These advancements require careful consideration of their ethical implications, including issues related to fairness, transparency, and the potential for misuse. Organizations must stay informed about technological developments and integrate ethical considerations into their decision-making processes, ensuring that their deception practices remain responsible and aligned with evolving standards.

Finally, fostering a culture of ethical awareness and compliance within an organization is vital for the responsible implementation of deception strategies. This involves not only adhering to legal and ethical guidelines but also promoting a proactive approach to ethics among all stakeholders involved in cybersecurity. Training and education programs can help ensure that employees and decision-makers understand the ethical implications of deception and are equipped to make informed choices. Additionally, establishing clear policies and procedures for the ethical deployment of deception, coupled with mechanisms for oversight and accountability, reinforces the organization's commitment to responsible practices.

In summary, the deployment of deception in cybersecurity necessitates a comprehensive approach that addresses a wide range of legal and ethical considerations. By navigating the complexities of privacy laws, consent, proportionality, societal impact, and technological advancements, organizations can implement deception strategies that are both effective and ethically sound. Continuous engagement with legal and ethical standards, coupled with a commitment to transparency and accountability, will ensure that deception practices contribute to enhanced security while respecting the rights and interests of all stakeholders.

CHAPTER 14:

To effectively integrate deception into incident response, it is crucial to understand the strategic application of deceptive tactics at each stage of the incident lifecycle. This involves a careful blend of technical implementation and operational procedures to ensure that deception tools enhance rather than complicate the response process.

When deploying deception techniques, the primary goal is to improve incident detection by creating traps that lure attackers away from critical systems. The successful implementation of such traps begins with the careful design of deceptive environments that closely mimic legitimate assets. These deceptive environments can include fake servers, databases, or network shares, all of which are designed to attract and engage attackers. For example, a decoy server might be set up to appear as if it holds sensitive data, thereby attracting attackers who are probing for valuable information. By engaging with these deceptive assets, attackers inadvertently reveal their presence and techniques, providing early warnings of an ongoing attack.

Once an incident is detected through these deceptive methods, the next critical step is to analyze the attacker's behavior. Deception tools provide a wealth of data that can be used to understand the nature of the attack and the tactics employed. This analysis can involve examining the interactions with deceptive assets, including the commands issued and the data accessed. For instance, if an attacker interacts with a honeypot designed to emulate a financial database, security analysts can review the specific queries made to determine what information the attacker sought and how they intended to exploit it. This detailed insight into attacker behavior is invaluable for shaping an effective response strategy and understanding the broader implications of the attack.

Incorporating deception into incident response also involves using these tools to mislead attackers and control their actions during an active security event. One effective technique is to redirect attackers from critical systems to controlled, isolated environments. For example, upon detecting an intruder, security teams might redirect them to a virtual environment that simulates the organization's network but contains only limited, non-sensitive information. This redirection not only prevents the attacker from accessing valuable assets but also provides additional time for the security team to respond and address the threat. Such strategies can significantly reduce the potential damage and minimize the disruption caused by the attack.

Furthermore, deception can play a pivotal role in post-incident analysis and recovery. The data collected from deceptive assets during an attack can be instrumental in understanding the full scope of the incident and refining the organization's security posture. For instance, analysis of attacker interactions with honeypots can reveal not only the specific methods used but also potential vulnerabilities within the organization's real systems that may have been exploited. This information can then be used to enhance defensive measures and improve incident response protocols.

Another critical aspect of using deception in incident response is ensuring that the deployment of deceptive techniques aligns with legal and ethical standards. It is essential to ensure that the use of deception does not inadvertently cause harm to innocent parties or violate privacy laws. This involves setting clear boundaries for the deployment of deceptive assets and ensuring that they are used in a manner that is consistent with organizational policies and legal requirements. Transparency is key in this regard, as security teams must be able to justify the use of deceptive techniques and demonstrate that they are employed in a responsible and ethical manner.

Effective communication and coordination among security teams are also crucial when integrating deception into incident response. Security professionals must be trained to recognize and interpret the signals generated by deceptive assets and to understand how these signals fit into the broader context of an ongoing incident. This requires not only technical expertise but also strong collaboration and coordination with other teams involved in incident response, including IT, legal, and management.

In summary, integrating deception into incident response provides a sophisticated approach to improving detection, analysis, and containment of cyber incidents. By carefully designing and deploying deceptive assets, organizations can enhance their ability to detect and understand attacks, mislead attackers, and minimize damage. The successful implementation of these techniques requires a strategic approach that balances technical, legal, and ethical considerations, as well as effective coordination among security teams. As the threat landscape continues to evolve, the role of deception in incident response will become increasingly important in maintaining robust cybersecurity defenses and safeguarding critical assets.

In the context of incident response, the integration of deception technologies can be further refined through the use of adaptive and dynamic deception techniques. These techniques involve tailoring deceptive elements based on real-time information about the attack and the behavior of the attacker. By employing adaptive deception, organizations can ensure that their deceptive measures remain effective even as the attacker's tactics evolve.

One approach to dynamic deception is the use of automated systems that adjust deceptive tactics based on observed attacker behavior. For example, if an attacker begins to display certain patterns or techniques, the deception tools can automatically adjust their configurations to better align with the evolving attack profile. This might include altering the appearance of decoy systems, modifying the data they present, or introducing new traps that address specific techniques being used by the attacker. The goal is to keep attackers engaged with deceptive elements that are continually changing, thereby making it more difficult for them to discern what is real and what is false.

Moreover, the use of deception in incident response extends to enhancing the forensic analysis of cyber incidents. During and after an attack, deceptive systems can provide critical information about the methods and tools used by attackers. For instance, if an attacker interacts with a honeypot designed to mimic a critical system, the data collected from this interaction can reveal the tools and techniques used, such as the specific malware or exploits employed. This detailed forensic information is invaluable for understanding how the attack was executed, which vulnerabilities were targeted, and how similar attacks might be prevented in the future.

In addition to providing insight into attacker methods, deception can also be employed to gather intelligence on broader threat landscapes. By analyzing the patterns of attack and the data collected from deceptive environments, security teams can identify trends and emerging threats. For instance, if multiple attacks are observed targeting similar deceptive assets, this may indicate a broader campaign or an emerging threat actor. This intelligence can then be used to inform and update broader security strategies and defensive measures.

Another important consideration in using deception for incident response is ensuring that the integration of these

CHAPTER 15:

In assessing the effectiveness of cybersecurity deception strategies, it is essential to delve into a nuanced examination of various qualitative and quantitative factors that can reveal the true impact of these measures. Beyond the initial metrics and benchmarks, understanding how these strategies function within the broader context of security operations provides deeper insights into their efficacy.

Evaluating deception involves not just looking at whether it detects attacks but also at how it influences the attacker's behavior and impacts overall security operations. One of the critical aspects to consider is the effectiveness of deception in changing the tactics and strategies employed by attackers. By analyzing patterns in attack methods before and after the implementation of deception strategies, one can discern whether the deception has led to a noticeable shift in attacker behavior. For instance, if attackers begin to focus on less critical or false targets, it indicates that the deception is successfully diverting their efforts away from valuable assets.

Furthermore, the adaptability of deception techniques to evolving threats is a crucial measure of their effectiveness. Deception strategies must be dynamic and capable of adjusting to new attack vectors and tactics. An effective deception strategy will include mechanisms for regular updates and modifications to its deceptive elements, ensuring that they remain relevant and convincing. Evaluating how frequently and effectively these updates are applied can provide insights into the long-term viability of the deception measures in place.

Another vital area of assessment is the integration of deception within the overall incident response and security operations framework. Deception should complement and enhance existing security measures rather than operate in isolation. Evaluating how well deception integrates with other security tools, such as intrusion detection systems and threat intelligence platforms, is essential. The goal is to ensure that deception contributes to a cohesive security strategy that maximizes overall effectiveness. This integration can be assessed by examining how deception tools interact with other systems, the ease with which they can be incorporated into existing workflows, and their impact on incident response times and accuracy.

The impact of deception on resource allocation and operational efficiency is also a significant consideration. While deception strategies can provide substantial benefits, they also require careful management to avoid resource strain. Evaluating the operational impact involves analyzing the resources required for the deployment, maintenance, and management of deception tools. It is important to balance the benefits of deception with its resource costs to ensure that it contributes positively to the security posture without overburdening the team or infrastructure.

The quality of the feedback and intelligence provided by deception strategies is another critical factor. Deception should yield actionable intelligence that can inform future security measures and enhance threat detection and response capabilities. Evaluating the quality of this intelligence involves assessing its relevance, accuracy, and usefulness in identifying and mitigating threats. This can be done by reviewing the types of insights generated through deception, such as patterns in attacker behavior, tools used, and potential vulnerabilities exploited. Effective deception should provide valuable data that can lead to improved security measures and threat mitigation strategies.

In addition to technical metrics, it is also essential to consider the human factors involved in deception. The effectiveness of deception can be influenced by how well it is understood and managed by the security team. Training and awareness play a crucial role in ensuring that the team can effectively deploy and respond to deception measures. Evaluating the team's readiness and understanding of deception strategies can provide insights into how well these measures are implemented and managed. This includes assessing training programs, documentation, and the overall knowledge of the security staff regarding deception techniques.

Case studies of organizations that have implemented deception strategies can offer valuable lessons and insights. By examining real-world examples, one can learn about the practical challenges and successes associated with deception. For instance, a case study might reveal how a particular organization used deception to successfully detect and mitigate a sophisticated attack or how adjustments to their deception strategy led to improved performance. These case studies provide a practical perspective on the effectiveness of different deception approaches and can guide future implementations.

Benchmarking against industry standards and best practices is also crucial for evaluating deception effectiveness. By comparing the performance of deception strategies with established benchmarks, organizations can gauge how their measures align with industry norms. This comparison can highlight strengths and areas for improvement, helping to set realistic goals and expectations for deception initiatives.

In conclusion, a comprehensive evaluation of cybersecurity deception strategies involves a multifaceted approach that considers not only detection and engagement metrics but also the integration, adaptability, and impact on overall security operations. By examining these factors, along with real-world case studies and industry benchmarks, organizations can gain a thorough understanding of the effectiveness of their deception measures and make informed decisions to refine and enhance their security posture.

Evaluating the effectiveness of cybersecurity deception is a complex process that requires a thorough understanding of both quantitative metrics and qualitative insights. To gain a comprehensive view of how well deception strategies are performing, one must consider multiple dimensions, including the depth of deception, its impact on security posture, and the overall efficiency of the response mechanisms.

One of the fundamental aspects to assess is the depth and complexity of the deception employed. The sophistication of deception techniques, such as honeypots and decoys, significantly influences their effectiveness. Evaluating this aspect involves analyzing how well the deception mimics real assets and systems. For instance, a highly effective deception strategy will incorporate elements that closely resemble legitimate operational systems, making it difficult for attackers to distinguish between real and fake. This requires a detailed examination of the design and deployment of deceptive elements to ensure they are convincing and capable of engaging sophisticated adversaries.

To assess how deception impacts the overall security posture, it is essential to evaluate the changes in attack patterns and the effectiveness of threat detection. Successful deception should lead to noticeable shifts in attacker behavior, such as an increase in the time attackers spend engaging with deceptive elements or a change in their attack vectors. By monitoring these behavioral changes, one can gauge whether the deception is effectively redirecting or slowing down attackers. Additionally, analyzing how deception affects the detection of real threats is crucial. Effective deception should not only distract or mislead attackers but also enhance the detection of genuine threats by providing additional data and insights.

Another critical component of the evaluation process is examining the efficiency of response mechanisms in the context of deception. This involves assessing how well incident response teams are able to integrate and act upon information derived from deceptive elements. Effective deception should not only provide valuable intelligence but also enable quicker and more accurate responses to real threats. Evaluating the efficiency of response mechanisms includes reviewing incident response times, the accuracy of threat identification, and the overall impact on containment and mitigation efforts.

Furthermore, the alignment of deception strategies with organizational goals and risk management objectives must be scrutinized. Effective deception should support and enhance the organization's broader security objectives, such as protecting critical assets and minimizing operational disruptions. Assessing this alignment involves analyzing whether the deception strategies are meeting the specific needs and risk profiles of the organization. For example, if a deception strategy is designed to protect sensitive data, it should be evaluated on how well it prevents data exfiltration and protects against targeted attacks.

It is also important to evaluate the cost-effectiveness of deception strategies. Implementing and maintaining deception techniques can be resource-intensive, so understanding the return on investment is crucial. This involves analyzing the costs associated with deploying and managing deception tools, as well as the benefits they provide in terms of threat detection, attacker diversion, and overall security enhancement. By comparing these costs with the tangible benefits and improvements in security posture, one can determine the overall value of the deception strategies.

Real-world case studies offer valuable insights into the practical application and effectiveness of deception strategies. By examining how different organizations have implemented and evaluated their deception measures, one can gain practical understanding and identify best practices. Case studies provide concrete examples of how deception has been used to detect and mitigate specific types of attacks, as well as how organizations have refined their approaches based on lessons learned. These examples can illustrate both successful outcomes and challenges faced, providing a more nuanced understanding of the effectiveness of deception in various contexts.

Benchmarking against industry standards and peer organizations can also provide a useful perspective on the effectiveness of deception strategies. By comparing the performance of one's own deception measures with those of similar organizations, one can identify areas for improvement and ensure that the strategies align with industry best practices. This benchmarking process can highlight strengths and weaknesses, offering a clearer view of how well the deception strategies are performing relative to industry norms.

Finally, continuous monitoring and iterative refinement of deception strategies are essential for maintaining their effectiveness over time. The threat landscape is constantly evolving, and so must the deception techniques employed. Regularly reviewing and updating deception measures based on new intelligence, emerging threats, and changes in the organization's risk profile ensures that the strategies remain effective and relevant. This ongoing evaluation process involves not only assessing current performance but also adapting and enhancing deception techniques to address new challenges and opportunities.

In conclusion, evaluating the effectiveness of cybersecurity deception strategies involves a multifaceted approach that includes assessing the depth and complexity of the deception, its impact on security posture, and the efficiency of response mechanisms. By considering these factors, along with real-world case studies, benchmarking, and continuous refinement, organizations can gain a comprehensive understanding of the performance of their deception measures and make informed decisions to enhance their overall security posture.

CHAPTER 16:

To construct an effective deception framework, it is crucial to delve deeper into the specifics of implementation and management strategies. Having established the foundational components such as objectives and resource allocation, the focus now shifts to the detailed design and operational aspects of the deception framework.

The design of a deception framework necessitates an intricate understanding of the organization's threat landscape and operational environment. Deception techniques, when implemented effectively, can significantly enhance threat detection and response capabilities. The selection of specific deceptive elements, such as honeypots, decoys, and bait systems, must be informed by a thorough analysis of potential attack vectors and the organization's existing security architecture.

Honeypots, for instance, are designed to attract and engage attackers by simulating vulnerabilities. These can be categorized into various types, including low-interaction, high-interaction, and hybrid honeypots, each serving different purposes. Low-interaction honeypots provide limited interaction with attackers, primarily gathering data on automated attack tools and techniques. High-interaction honeypots, on the other hand, offer a more immersive environment, allowing attackers to interact with a simulated system in a way that mimics real-world conditions. Hybrid honeypots combine elements of both to balance between interaction depth and operational complexity.

When integrating honeypots into the deception framework, strategic placement is vital. For instance, deploying honeypots in areas that are likely targets for attackers, such as exposed network segments or critical infrastructure components, can increase the likelihood of detecting malicious activities. Additionally, these honeypots must be designed to blend seamlessly with legitimate systems to avoid detection and maintain their effectiveness. This involves configuring them with realistic operating systems, applications, and data.

Decoys, another critical component of the deception framework, serve to mislead attackers and divert their attention away from genuine assets. The deployment of decoys involves creating fake but convincing systems and services within the network. These can include fake servers, databases, and even entire network segments that appear operational but are designed to mislead and trap attackers. Effective decoys are often equipped with simulated data and functionalities that reflect the organization's real systems, thereby enhancing their credibility.

The design of decoys should also consider the integration with other security measures. For example, decoys can be configured to interact with the organization's Security Information and Event Management (SIEM) system, providing valuable insights into attacker behavior and tactics. This integration allows for the correlation of deceptive activities with other security events, providing a comprehensive view of the threat landscape.

Bait systems are another innovative approach within the deception framework. Baiting involves creating enticing targets that lure attackers into interacting with deceptive elements. This can include fake credentials, sensitive-looking documents, or even fraudulent communication channels. The purpose of bait systems is to attract attackers into engaging with deceptive environments where their actions can be monitored and analyzed.

Operational management of the deception framework requires ongoing attention to ensure its effectiveness and relevance. Regular updates and maintenance are essential to keep the deception techniques aligned with evolving threat landscapes and organizational changes. This includes periodically reviewing and updating deceptive configurations, incorporating new threat intelligence, and adapting to changes in the organization's network and infrastructure.

Additionally, monitoring and analyzing the performance of the deception framework is crucial for understanding its impact and effectiveness. This involves collecting and examining data from deceptive elements, such as honeypots and decoys, to assess their effectiveness in detecting and misleading attackers. Key performance indicators (KPIs) should be established to measure the success of the deception strategy, such as the number of detected attacks, the quality of intelligence gathered, and the impact on overall threat detection and response.

Feedback loops play an important role in refining and improving the deception framework. Insights gained from monitoring activities and performance metrics should be used to make informed adjustments to the deception techniques and strategies. This iterative process ensures that the deception framework remains effective and continues to meet the organization's security objectives.

Furthermore, establishing clear communication protocols and collaboration mechanisms within the organization is essential for the successful implementation and management of the deception framework. This includes ensuring that all relevant stakeholders, such as IT teams, security personnel, and management, are informed about the deception strategy and its objectives. Effective communication facilitates coordination and ensures that deceptive insights are integrated into broader security operations and incident response efforts.

In conclusion, building a comprehensive deception framework involves a detailed approach to designing, implementing, and managing deception techniques. By strategically selecting and deploying deceptive elements, integrating them with existing security measures, and continuously monitoring and refining their effectiveness, organizations can enhance their ability to detect and respond to cyber threats. The success of a deception framework hinges on its alignment with organizational goals, its adaptability to evolving threats, and its seamless integration with the overall security infrastructure.

The final stage in developing a comprehensive deception framework involves the ongoing evaluation and adaptation of the deception strategy to ensure its continued effectiveness. As organizations grow and evolve, so too do the threats they face and the technologies they employ. Thus, maintaining an agile and responsive deception framework is crucial for sustaining its value over time.

A key aspect of this phase is establishing a robust evaluation process. To evaluate the effectiveness of the deception framework, organizations must engage in regular and systematic assessments. This entails measuring how well the deception elements are performing against predefined objectives and metrics. The effectiveness of the deception strategy can be gauged through several indicators, including the frequency and type of interactions with deceptive elements, the quality of intelligence collected, and the overall impact on threat detection and incident response.

One effective approach to evaluation is conducting periodic penetration tests and red team exercises. These tests simulate real-world attack scenarios and provide insights into how well the deception framework withstands and mitigates such threats. During these exercises, the deception components are assessed for their ability to attract, engage, and mislead attackers. The results of these tests offer valuable feedback on the effectiveness of the deception elements and highlight areas for improvement.

In addition to formal assessments, continuous monitoring plays a crucial role in maintaining the effectiveness of the deception framework. Implementing real-time monitoring tools allows organizations to track interactions with deceptive elements and collect data on attacker behavior. This real-time data can be analyzed to detect patterns, identify emerging threats, and adjust deception techniques as needed. The insights gained from continuous monitoring also inform updates to the deception framework, ensuring it remains relevant and effective in the face of evolving threats.

Integration with broader security operations is another critical factor in the ongoing success of the deception framework. Deception strategies should not operate in isolation but should be seamlessly incorporated into the organization's overall security posture. This includes integrating deceptive elements with threat intelligence platforms, Security Information and Event Management (SIEM) systems, and incident response workflows. By correlating data from deception elements with other security data sources, organizations can enhance their understanding of the threat landscape and improve their response capabilities.

Collaboration and communication within the organization are essential for the successful implementation and management of the deception framework. Engaging stakeholders from various departments, including IT, security, and management, ensures that the deception strategy is aligned with organizational objectives and that its insights are effectively utilized. Regular updates and briefings on the performance of the deception framework help keep all relevant parties informed and engaged, fostering a collaborative approach to security.

Another important consideration is the ethical and legal implications of deploying deception techniques. As organizations implement and refine their deception strategies, they must remain vigilant about compliance with relevant laws and regulations. This includes ensuring that deception practices do not inadvertently infringe on privacy rights or violate legal boundaries. It is also crucial to maintain transparency with stakeholders about the use of deception techniques and their objectives, thereby upholding ethical standards and fostering trust.

To support the continuous improvement of the deception framework, organizations should establish feedback mechanisms that facilitate the collection of insights and lessons learned. After each evaluation or incident response exercise, conducting a thorough review and analysis of the results helps identify strengths, weaknesses, and opportunities for enhancement. This iterative process of feedback and refinement ensures that the deception framework evolves in response to new challenges and emerging threats.

In conclusion, the ongoing management and refinement of a deception framework are integral to its long-term success. By implementing systematic evaluation processes, leveraging real-time monitoring, integrating with broader security operations, and addressing ethical and legal considerations, organizations can maintain an effective and adaptive deception strategy. This approach not only enhances the organization's ability to detect and respond to cyber threats but also ensures that the deception framework continues to align with organizational goals and risk profiles. Through continuous improvement and proactive management, organizations can maximize the value of their deception efforts and strengthen their overall security posture.

CHAPTER 17:

To fully appreciate the role of deception in threat intelligence, it is essential to explore how deception tools can be structured to maximize their value. The design and implementation of these tools must align with the specific objectives of threat intelligence gathering. Deception techniques are not merely supplementary; they are a critical component in creating a layered security approach that offers deeper insights into adversary behaviors and intentions.

One effective method for integrating deception into threat intelligence involves the deployment of honeypots and honeynets that are carefully designed to emulate real systems and networks. Honeypots are systems that appear vulnerable and are intentionally exposed to attract attackers. They serve as controlled environments where interactions with attackers can be observed and analyzed. Honeynets, on the other hand, are networks of interconnected honeypots that create a more extensive and realistic environment for attackers to interact with. This extended network setup allows for a broader observation of attack behaviors and strategies.

Incorporating data from these honeypots and honeynets into threat intelligence platforms involves a multi-step process. First, data collected from these deceptive systems must be structured and categorized to facilitate integration with other threat intelligence sources. This involves setting up protocols for data extraction and normalization, ensuring that the information can be seamlessly ingested into threat intelligence platforms. For instance, logs and alerts generated by honeypots need to be parsed and correlated with other security event data, such as those from intrusion detection systems or endpoint protection solutions.

Once the data is integrated, it becomes crucial to apply analytical methods to derive actionable insights. Threat intelligence platforms can use machine learning algorithms and behavioral analytics to identify patterns and anomalies within the data. By analyzing interactions with deceptive systems, these platforms can uncover previously unknown attack vectors or methods used by threat actors. For example, if a honeypot designed to simulate a critical infrastructure system is frequently targeted by a specific type of exploit, this information can be used to update threat intelligence reports and adjust defensive measures accordingly.

Moreover, deception data can significantly enhance the development of threat actor profiles. Understanding the specific tactics, techniques, and procedures (TTPs) used by adversaries is essential for creating accurate threat actor profiles. When attackers engage with deceptive systems, their actions can be analyzed to refine these profiles. For instance, if an attacker uses a particular set of tools or follows a specific pattern of behavior when interacting with a honeypot, this data can be used to build a more detailed profile of that attacker or their group. These profiles are invaluable for predicting future attack behaviors and preparing defenses in advance.

The application of deception also allows organizations to validate and refine their existing threat intelligence assumptions. For example, if an organization hypothesizes that a particular threat group is targeting specific vulnerabilities, deploying a deceptive system that mirrors these vulnerabilities can provide real-world data to confirm or refute the hypothesis. This validation process helps ensure that threat intelligence is based on empirical evidence rather than assumptions, leading to more effective and targeted security strategies.

Another important aspect of integrating deception with threat intelligence is the enhancement of incident response capabilities. By providing real-time data on attacker behaviors and tactics, deception techniques can improve the accuracy of incident detection and response. When an attacker engages with a deceptive element, the information gathered can be used to identify the nature of the attack, the tools being used, and the potential impact. This real-time intelligence enables more informed decision-making during security incidents, allowing for quicker containment and remediation actions.

In addition, integrating deception data with threat intelligence platforms fosters a more proactive approach to cybersecurity. By continuously monitoring and analyzing deceptive environments, organizations can gain early warning of emerging threats and attack trends. This proactive stance allows for the adjustment of security measures before an actual attack occurs, improving overall resilience and reducing the likelihood of successful breaches.

Finally, the integration of deception into threat intelligence strategies also supports collaboration among different security teams. The insights gained from deceptive interactions can be shared with threat intelligence analysts, incident response teams, and other stakeholders to ensure a unified approach to threat management. This collaborative effort helps to synthesize information from various sources, providing a comprehensive view of the threat landscape and enabling more effective coordination in addressing potential security challenges.

In essence, the integration of deception with threat intelligence represents a strategic advancement in cybersecurity. By leveraging deceptive techniques to gather detailed data on attacker behaviors and integrating this information into threat intelligence platforms, organizations can gain a deeper understanding of the threat landscape. This approach enhances threat forecasting, validates existing assumptions, and improves incident response capabilities, ultimately leading to a more robust and informed security posture.

When considering the intersection of deception and threat intelligence, the integration of deceptive tactics with threat intelligence platforms requires careful planning and execution. Effective integration hinges on the seamless flow of data between deceptive elements and intelligence systems, and the ability to analyze and act on this data in real time.

A key component of this integration is the establishment of a robust data collection framework. Deceptive systems, such as honeypots or decoy networks, generate a wealth of information when interacted with by attackers. This data, however, is often voluminous and varied, making it essential to have a system in place to capture, store, and manage it effectively. Sophisticated data collection mechanisms must be employed to ensure that all relevant interactions are logged and that data integrity is maintained throughout the process.

Once data is collected, the next step involves its normalization and enrichment to make it suitable for threat intelligence platforms. Normalization involves converting the raw data into a standardized format that can be easily ingested by these platforms. Enrichment, on the other hand, adds contextual information to the raw data, such as associating IP addresses with known threat actor profiles or linking observed tactics to specific attack methodologies. This step is crucial for transforming raw data into actionable intelligence.

The integration of deceptive data with threat intelligence platforms also requires advanced correlation techniques. By correlating data from deceptive systems with information from other sources—such as network traffic logs, endpoint alerts, or external threat feeds—organizations can achieve a more comprehensive view of the threat landscape. This correlation process enables the identification of patterns and trends that might not be evident when analyzing deceptive data in isolation. For example, an increase in activity targeting a particular honeypot might correlate with a spike in activity related to a specific threat actor or attack type observed in broader threat intelligence feeds.

Another important aspect of integrating deception with threat intelligence is the continuous updating of threat models and indicators of compromise (IOCs). As deceptive systems capture new attack methods and tactics, these insights should be used to refine and update existing threat models. This dynamic approach ensures that threat intelligence remains current and relevant, reflecting the latest developments in attacker techniques and strategies. Updating IOCs based on insights gained from deceptive environments also improves the accuracy of threat detection mechanisms and helps to anticipate future attack trends.

The use of deception in threat intelligence can also be leveraged to enhance threat hunting activities. Threat hunters rely on a combination of threat intelligence, behavioral analysis, and investigative techniques to proactively search for signs of compromise within an organization's environment. Deception data can provide valuable clues and context that support threat hunting efforts, enabling hunters to focus on specific areas of interest or adjust their search strategies based on the latest insights. For instance, if a deceptive system reveals a new attack vector or exploit method, threat hunters can use this information to target their investigations and identify potential indicators of compromise that might otherwise go unnoticed.

Moreover, deception techniques can be instrumental in validating and testing existing threat intelligence hypotheses. For example, if an organization believes that a particular threat actor is targeting specific vulnerabilities, deploying deceptive systems that mimic these vulnerabilities allows for empirical testing of this hypothesis. The interactions observed in these deceptive environments can either confirm or challenge the initial assumptions, leading to more accurate and actionable intelligence.

Collaboration and communication between different security teams are also enhanced through the integration of deception and threat intelligence. By sharing insights gained from deceptive systems with incident response teams, threat analysts, and other stakeholders, organizations can foster a more coordinated approach to threat management. This collaborative effort ensures that all relevant parties are informed about emerging threats and can take appropriate actions based on the latest intelligence.

In addition, the integration of deception into threat intelligence platforms facilitates a more proactive security posture. By continuously monitoring and analyzing deceptive environments, organizations can gain early warning of emerging threats and adjust their defenses accordingly. This proactive approach allows for timely responses to potential security challenges and helps to minimize the impact of successful attacks.

Ultimately, the intersection of deception and threat intelligence represents a powerful synergy that enhances an organization's ability to understand, detect, and respond to cyber threats. By integrating deceptive techniques with threat intelligence platforms, organizations can achieve a deeper understanding of attacker behaviors, improve threat detection and response capabilities, and maintain a more resilient security posture. The insights gained from deceptive systems not only enrich threat intelligence but also support a proactive and adaptive approach to cybersecurity, ensuring that defenses remain effective against evolving threats.

CHAPTER 18:

Examining real-world applications of deception strategies provides a clearer understanding of their effectiveness in various cybersecurity contexts. For instance, consider the case of a multinational corporation facing frequent and sophisticated attacks aimed at compromising its intellectual property. This organization utilized a deceptive approach by creating a network of high-fidelity honeypots designed to simulate critical systems and sensitive data repositories.

These honeypots were not merely isolated traps; they were embedded within the company's actual network infrastructure, mimicking the real systems closely. The deception involved creating fake databases and mimicking genuine network traffic patterns to lure attackers into engaging with these decoys. By analyzing the interactions with these honeypots, the organization gained crucial insights into the attacker's tactics, techniques, and procedures (TTPs).

The key benefit derived from this approach was the detailed intelligence on the attackers' methods and preferences. For example, the honeypots revealed specific tools and techniques used by the attackers, as well as their methods for trying to exfiltrate data. This intelligence allowed the company to refine its defensive measures, address previously unknown vulnerabilities, and enhance its overall security posture. The integration of these insights into the company's broader threat intelligence strategy facilitated a more proactive and adaptive defense.

In another example, a government agency tasked with

safeguarding sensitive national security information employed deception to counter persistent cyber espionage attempts. This agency implemented a comprehensive deception framework that included a combination of fake communication channels, deceptive data sources, and misleading network structures. These decoys were designed to mimic real operational environments and attract adversaries.

The deception strategy proved effective in several ways. It not only helped in detecting unauthorized access attempts but also provided a means to assess the capabilities and intentions of the attackers. For instance, interactions with the fake communication channels revealed that attackers were using advanced social engineering techniques to gain access. This information was critical in developing targeted training programs for personnel and improving the agency's internal security protocols.

Moreover, the use of deceptive data sources allowed the agency to trace the origins and methods of the espionage attempts more accurately. By analyzing how attackers interacted with these decoys, the agency could identify the specific tactics employed and adapt its defensive strategies accordingly. This case underscores the strategic value of deception in gathering actionable intelligence and enhancing organizational resilience against sophisticated threats.

A different scenario highlights the application of deception in mitigating insider threats within a large financial institution. The organization faced significant challenges related to potential malicious activities by employees who had access to sensitive financial information. To address this, a deception strategy was employed that included creating fake financial transactions and simulated internal alerts.

These deceptive elements were carefully integrated into the institution's financial systems to mimic real transactions and alerts. The objective was to detect any anomalous behavior that might indicate malicious intent or insider threat activities. By monitoring interactions with these deceptive elements, the institution could identify and investigate suspicious activities that could be indicative of insider threats.

The success of this approach was evident in its ability to uncover several previously undetected cases of insider misconduct. The fake transactions and alerts not only helped in identifying potential threats but also provided valuable insights into the methods and motivations of the insiders. This information was used to enhance the institution's internal monitoring processes and strengthen its overall security framework.

In yet another instance, a major e-commerce company utilized deception techniques to protect its online platform from a series of targeted attacks. The attackers aimed to exploit vulnerabilities in the platform to gain unauthorized access to customer data and payment information. The company's response involved deploying a range of deceptive measures, including fake payment processing systems and fictitious customer accounts.

These deceptive elements were designed to attract and mislead attackers, providing valuable intelligence on their tactics and techniques. For example, interactions with the fake payment systems revealed specific tools and methods used by the attackers to attempt data exfiltration. This intelligence was crucial in identifying and addressing vulnerabilities in the actual e-commerce platform, thereby enhancing the company's ability to defend against future attacks.

The effectiveness of this approach was demonstrated by the company's improved ability to detect and mitigate attacks in real time. The insights gained from the deceptive measures allowed the company to implement targeted security enhancements and better protect its customers' sensitive information.

Each of these case studies illustrates the diverse ways in which deception can be employed to address various cybersecurity challenges. The strategic use of deceptive techniques provides valuable insights into attacker behaviors, enhances the detection of malicious activities, and contributes to a more robust overall security posture. By analyzing these real-world examples, organizations can gain practical insights into the effective implementation of deception strategies and apply these lessons to strengthen their own cybersecurity defenses.

In examining the implementation of deception strategies across diverse scenarios, it's crucial to consider the nuances and outcomes that define their success. A case involving a healthcare organization grappling with a surge in ransomware attacks illustrates the adaptive use of deceptive tactics. This organization, which managed a vast array of sensitive patient data, was targeted by attackers seeking to encrypt files and demand ransoms. To counter this threat, the organization deployed a range of deceptive mechanisms, including fake patient records and simulated critical system alerts.

These deceptive elements were carefully integrated into the organization's actual data systems, designed to attract the ransomware operators without compromising real patient information. By embedding fake records within the system, the organization aimed to divert the attackers' attention and resources away from genuine data. The simulated alerts and notifications were crafted to appear as though critical systems were being compromised, thus creating a misleading scenario that hampered the attackers' efforts to assess and exploit vulnerabilities.

The impact of these deception techniques was significant. The healthcare organization observed a reduction in the number of successful ransomware infections, as attackers were misled into focusing on the decoys. Furthermore, the deceptive measures provided valuable insights into the attackers' strategies, including their methods for identifying and targeting critical data. This intelligence was used to refine the organization's overall security posture and develop more robust defenses against ransomware threats.

Another compelling case involves a technology firm that faced a series of sophisticated phishing attacks targeting its executives and high-value targets. The firm implemented a deception strategy involving fake executive email accounts and fraudulent communication channels. These decoys were designed to mimic the real communication patterns and styles used by the company's executives, making it difficult for attackers to distinguish between genuine and deceptive emails.

The deployment of these deceptive email accounts achieved several objectives. First, it provided a controlled environment in which to observe and analyze the attackers' tactics and techniques. By studying how attackers interacted with these decoys, the firm gained insights into their phishing methodologies, including their approach to social engineering and data exfiltration. Second, the deceptive emails helped in identifying compromised credentials and potential insider threats, allowing the firm to take corrective actions swiftly.

The effectiveness of this approach was evident in the firm's improved ability to detect and respond to phishing attempts. The data collected from the deceptive email interactions enabled the company to enhance its phishing detection mechanisms and train its employees on recognizing and handling similar threats. This case highlights the value of deception in not only thwarting attacks but also in providing actionable intelligence for strengthening defenses.

In another instance, a financial services firm employed deception techniques to address a growing problem of fraudulent transactions and account takeovers. The firm implemented a range of deceptive measures, including fake accounts and simulated transaction patterns, to attract and identify malicious actors attempting to exploit the system. These deceptive elements were designed to mimic real financial activities, creating an environment where attackers could be monitored and analyzed.

The use of deceptive accounts and transactions yielded valuable insights into the techniques and tools used by fraudsters. For instance, the firm identified specific patterns of behavior associated with fraudulent activities, such as the timing and frequency of transactions. This information was used to enhance the firm's fraud detection algorithms and implement more stringent controls to prevent future occurrences.

The impact of these deception techniques extended beyond immediate threat detection. By understanding the methods employed by fraudsters, the firm was able to develop more effective countermeasures and improve its overall fraud prevention strategy. This case underscores the importance of deception not only in identifying and mitigating current threats but also in informing long-term security improvements.

Lastly, a telecommunications company faced challenges related to distributed denial-of-service (DDoS) attacks aimed at disrupting its network services. The company deployed a deception strategy that involved creating fake network services and infrastructure to divert the attention of attackers. These deceptive elements were designed to simulate real network traffic and services, creating a misleading environment for the attackers.

The use of deceptive network services had a profound impact on the company's ability to manage and mitigate DDoS attacks. By attracting the attackers to the decoys, the company was able to protect its genuine network infrastructure and minimize service disruptions. Additionally, the deceptive network services provided valuable data on the nature and scale of the DDoS attacks, allowing the company to refine its mitigation strategies and improve its overall resilience against similar threats.

These case studies illustrate the diverse and impactful ways in which deception techniques can be employed to address various cybersecurity challenges. The strategic implementation of deceptive measures provides organizations with valuable insights into attacker behaviors, enhances threat detection capabilities, and contributes to a more robust and adaptive security posture. By analyzing these real-world examples, it becomes clear that deception is not merely a defensive tactic but a vital component of a comprehensive cybersecurity strategy.

CHAPTER 19:

Developing a robust skill set in cybersecurity deception involves a multifaceted approach that integrates both theoretical knowledge and practical application. To effectively master deception strategies, one must navigate through various stages of learning and practice, ensuring that both foundational principles and advanced techniques are well understood and applied.

A critical aspect of skill development in this field is the engagement with structured educational programs that focus specifically on cybersecurity deception. These programs typically offer a blend of theoretical frameworks and hands-on labs, enabling practitioners to grasp the intricate dynamics of deception in cybersecurity. Understanding the principles of deception, such as creating and managing decoys, setting traps, and employing honeypots, forms the bedrock of effective strategy implementation. Educational institutions and online platforms often provide courses tailored to these needs, ranging from introductory lessons to advanced technical training.

Moreover, professional certifications serve as a benchmark for knowledge and competency in cybersecurity deception. Certifications like the Certified Information Systems Security Professional (CISSP) and Certified Ethical Hacker (CEH) cover a broad spectrum of security topics, including deception techniques. More specialized certifications that focus on penetration testing or threat intelligence delve deeper into how deception can be used to detect and mitigate attacks. These certifications not only validate one's expertise but also signal to employers and clients a commitment to maintaining high standards in the field.

Hands-on experience is equally vital. Engaging in real-world simulations and practical exercises allows practitioners to apply theoretical knowledge in controlled environments. These simulations often recreate various attack scenarios, offering a practical platform to deploy and test deception strategies. This experiential learning is crucial for understanding the effectiveness of different deception techniques and for refining one's ability to adapt strategies to emerging threats. Labs and simulations can be accessed through specialized training programs or virtual environments designed to mimic real-world conditions.

To stay at the forefront of deception technology and techniques, continuous learning and professional development are indispensable. The cybersecurity landscape is dynamic, with new threats and advancements emerging regularly. Subscribing to industry publications, attending conferences, and participating in webinars provide insights into the latest trends and developments in deception. These resources offer opportunities to learn from industry leaders and to stay updated on innovative approaches and tools.

Research and development also play a significant role in advancing one's expertise in cybersecurity deception. Many organizations and academic institutions conduct research focused on refining deception techniques and evaluating their effectiveness. Engaging in or following such research provides exposure to cutting-edge strategies and contributes to a deeper understanding of how deception can be effectively implemented. Participating in collaborative research projects or case studies offers practical insights into how these strategies are applied in various contexts.

Networking within the cybersecurity community further

enhances expertise. Building relationships with peers, mentors, and industry experts can provide valuable perspectives on best practices and emerging trends. Networking opportunities are available through industry events, professional organizations, and online forums. These interactions facilitate the exchange of knowledge and experiences, helping practitioners to gain new insights and to refine their approaches to deception.

In addition to formal education and networking, self-assessment and continuous improvement are essential. Regularly evaluating one's skills and knowledge through self-assessment tools or peer reviews helps identify areas for development. Setting personal learning goals and seeking constructive feedback from colleagues or mentors can guide further growth and proficiency. This ongoing commitment to self-improvement ensures that practitioners remain adept at employing deception techniques effectively.

Lastly, practical application of skills in diverse scenarios is key to mastering deception strategies. By actively applying techniques in various contexts, practitioners gain a nuanced understanding of how different methods perform under different conditions. This hands-on experience helps in developing the ability to tailor strategies to specific threats and organizational needs, ultimately leading to more effective implementation and management of deception measures.

In summary, developing expertise in cybersecurity deception requires a comprehensive approach that combines formal education, professional certifications, hands-on practice, continuous learning, and networking. By engaging with structured educational programs, obtaining relevant certifications, participating in practical simulations, staying informed about technological advancements, and committing to ongoing self-improvement, practitioners can build the skills necessary to effectively implement and manage deception strategies. This multifaceted approach ensures that cybersecurity professionals are well-equipped to address the evolving challenges in the field of deception.

Developing expertise in cybersecurity deception is a multifaceted journey that requires dedication, continual learning, and practical experience. To effectively implement and manage deception strategies, one must not only understand the theoretical underpinnings but also apply them in real-world contexts. Building a robust skill set involves several interconnected elements that enhance both knowledge and practical ability.

To begin, gaining foundational knowledge through structured educational programs is essential. These programs often provide a comprehensive introduction to the principles of deception in cybersecurity. They cover critical concepts such as the design and deployment of honeypots, the creation of misleading signals to confuse attackers, and the management of deceptive traps. Engaging in coursework from reputable institutions or online platforms can offer a thorough grounding in these areas. Advanced courses delve deeper into specific techniques and strategies, enabling practitioners to tailor their deception methods to different threat landscapes.

In addition to formal education, obtaining relevant certifications can significantly bolster one's credentials in cybersecurity deception. Certifications such as the Certified Information Systems Security Professional (CISSP) and Certified Ethical Hacker (CEH) encompass a broad range of security topics, including deception. More specialized certifications, such as those focused on penetration testing or advanced threat intelligence, can provide deeper insights into how deception can be employed to identify and mitigate cyber threats. These certifications not only validate one's expertise but also signal a commitment to staying current with industry standards and practices.

Hands-on experience is a critical component of developing

deception skills. Participating in practical exercises and simulations allows practitioners to apply theoretical knowledge in a controlled environment. These simulations often mimic real-world attack scenarios, providing an opportunity to deploy and test various deception techniques. For instance, setting up a honeypot in a simulated network environment enables practitioners to observe how attackers interact with deceptive elements and to refine their strategies based on these observations. This practical application helps in understanding the effectiveness of different techniques and in adapting them to real-world situations.

Continuous learning and professional development are vital for staying abreast of advancements in deception technology and techniques. The field of cybersecurity is dynamic, with new threats and innovations emerging regularly. Subscribing to industry publications, attending conferences, and participating in webinars are effective ways to stay informed about the latest trends and developments. These resources provide valuable insights into new approaches and tools, as well as opportunities to learn from leading experts in the field. Engaging in these activities ensures that practitioners remain up-to-date with cutting-edge strategies and technologies.

Research and development play an essential role in advancing expertise in deception. Many organizations and academic institutions conduct research focused on improving deception techniques and evaluating their effectiveness. Following or participating in such research provides exposure to the latest findings and contributes to a deeper understanding of how deception can be applied in various contexts. Collaborative research projects and case studies offer practical insights into real-world applications and help refine deception strategies based on empirical evidence.

Networking with peers and industry experts is another important aspect of skill development. Building relationships within the cybersecurity community can provide valuable perspectives on best practices and emerging trends. Networking opportunities are available through industry events, professional organizations, and online forums. Engaging with other professionals allows for the exchange of knowledge and experiences, which can help in refining one's approaches to deception and in gaining new insights into effective techniques.

Self-assessment and continuous improvement are crucial for mastering deception skills. Regularly evaluating one's knowledge and skills through self-assessment tools or peer reviews helps identify areas for development. Setting personal learning goals and seeking feedback from colleagues or mentors can guide further growth and proficiency. This ongoing commitment to self-improvement ensures that practitioners are well-equipped to address evolving challenges in the field of cybersecurity deception.

Finally, applying deception techniques in diverse scenarios is essential for developing a nuanced understanding of their effectiveness. By actively implementing strategies in various contexts, practitioners can gain insights into how different methods perform under different conditions. This hands-on experience helps in tailoring deception techniques to specific threats and organizational needs, ultimately leading to more effective implementation and management of deception measures.

In conclusion, developing expertise in cybersecurity deception involves a comprehensive approach that combines formal education, certifications, hands-on experience, continuous learning, and networking. By engaging with educational programs, obtaining relevant certifications, participating in practical simulations, staying informed about technological advancements, and committing to ongoing self-improvement, practitioners can build the skills necessary to effectively implement and manage deception strategies. This multifaceted approach ensures that cybersecurity professionals are well-prepared to address the complex and evolving challenges in the realm of deception.

CHAPTER 20:

As I delve further into the future trends in cybersecurity deception, it becomes evident that the integration of advanced technologies will reshape the landscape of defensive strategies. The role of artificial intelligence (AI) in this evolution cannot be overstated. AI is expected to significantly enhance the sophistication and efficacy of deceptive tactics by introducing more adaptive and responsive mechanisms. This advancement stems from AI's capacity to process and analyze large volumes of data, enabling it to identify patterns and anomalies that might elude human detection.

In practical terms, AI-powered deception tools can create highly realistic and dynamic environments that mimic genuine systems with a remarkable degree of fidelity. For instance, AI can be used to develop honeypots that not only attract attackers but also simulate complex interactions that mirror those of a real network. This heightened realism can increase the likelihood of detecting and analyzing sophisticated attack methods, providing valuable insights into attacker behavior. Furthermore, AI algorithms can continuously evolve based on ongoing interactions with attackers, adapting deceptive tactics in real-time to counteract emerging threats and techniques.

Machine learning, as a subset of AI, plays a complementary role by enabling systems to learn from past experiences and improve their responses over time. This capability allows for the development of self-improving deceptive systems that can adapt to the changing tactics of cyber adversaries. For example, machine learning models can be trained on historical attack data to recognize new patterns and anomalies. As a result, these models can generate predictive insights that inform the deployment of deception resources in a more targeted and strategic manner. By leveraging machine learning, organizations can enhance their ability to anticipate and respond to sophisticated attack methods, thereby strengthening their overall cybersecurity posture.

Automation is another pivotal trend that will shape the future of cybersecurity deception. The increasing complexity of IT environments and the volume of cyber threats necessitate a more streamlined and efficient approach to managing deception strategies. Automation facilitates this by enabling the deployment, management, and orchestration of deception tools with minimal manual intervention. Automated systems can dynamically adjust deception tactics based on real-time threat intelligence, ensuring that defensive measures remain agile and responsive to evolving attack vectors.

One of the most significant advantages of automation in deception is its ability to scale deception efforts across large and complex environments. For instance, automated scripts and workflows can deploy and manage numerous honeypots, decoys, and traps simultaneously, ensuring comprehensive coverage and reducing the risk of gaps in defense. Additionally, automation allows for the rapid and consistent execution of deceptive measures, which is crucial for maintaining an effective defense against persistent and sophisticated threats.

As these technologies converge, we can anticipate the emergence of integrated deception platforms that combine AI, machine learning, and automation into a cohesive solution. These platforms will offer a comprehensive toolkit for cybersecurity professionals, enabling them to implement sophisticated deception strategies with greater efficiency and effectiveness. For example, an integrated platform might use AI to analyze incoming threats, machine learning to adapt deceptive tactics, and automation to deploy and manage deception resources. Such platforms will not only enhance the capabilities of deception strategies but also streamline their management and execution.

The future of deception also involves addressing new challenges posed by advanced persistent threats (APTs) and zero-day vulnerabilities. As cyber adversaries develop increasingly sophisticated tactics, deception strategies will need to be more adaptable and resilient. This may involve incorporating elements of behavioral analysis and threat intelligence to identify and deceive advanced attackers who employ stealthy methods. By integrating deception with other security measures, such as threat hunting and incident response, organizations can create a multi-layered defense approach that effectively counters sophisticated threats.

Moreover, the rise of quantum computing presents both opportunities and challenges for cybersecurity deception. Quantum computing has the potential to disrupt current encryption methods and enhance data processing capabilities. In response, deception strategies will need to evolve to address the unique threats posed by quantum computing. This could involve developing new types of deceptive technologies that are effective in a quantum-enabled environment or exploring ways to leverage quantum computing for defensive purposes.

Ethical considerations and regulatory compliance will also be critical in shaping the future of cybersecurity deception. As deception techniques become more advanced, it is essential to ensure that their deployment adheres to ethical standards and legal requirements. This includes addressing concerns related to privacy, data protection, and the potential for unintended consequences. Developing clear guidelines and best practices for the ethical use of deception will be crucial in maintaining trust and ensuring that deception strategies are used responsibly and effectively.

In conclusion, the future of cybersecurity deception will be significantly influenced by advancements in artificial intelligence, machine learning, and automation. These technologies will enhance the sophistication and effectiveness of deception strategies, enabling more proactive and adaptive defense mechanisms. As the threat landscape continues to evolve, deception techniques will need to adapt to address new challenges and integrate with other security measures. Ethical considerations and regulatory compliance will play an essential role in guiding the development and deployment of future deception strategies. By staying informed about these trends and actively engaging with emerging technologies, cybersecurity professionals can effectively prepare for and navigate the evolving landscape of cybersecurity deception.

As I explore the trajectory of cybersecurity deception, the integration of advanced technologies, particularly artificial intelligence (AI), machine learning, and automation, emerges as a critical factor in shaping its future. These advancements not only promise to enhance the sophistication of deceptive strategies but also bring new opportunities and challenges to the field.

Artificial intelligence is poised to revolutionize deception tactics by enabling the creation of highly adaptive and realistic deceptive environments. AI's capacity for deep data analysis and pattern recognition allows for the development of dynamic deception tools that can simulate real-world scenarios with unparalleled accuracy. By leveraging AI, cybersecurity professionals can craft honeypots and decoys that not only mimic genuine systems but also respond to interactions in a manner that closely resembles actual operational environments. This increased realism can significantly improve the likelihood of detecting and analyzing advanced threats, as attackers are more likely to engage with these convincingly realistic decoys. Moreover, AI-driven systems can continuously learn and adapt based on ongoing interactions, allowing them to evolve in response to emerging attack techniques and methodologies. This adaptive capability ensures that deception strategies remain effective against increasingly sophisticated adversaries.

Machine learning, a subset of AI, contributes to this evolution by enabling systems to learn from historical attack data and improve their detection and response mechanisms over time. Through training on large datasets, machine learning algorithms can identify patterns and anomalies that may indicate malicious activity. As these models are exposed to more data and interactions, they refine their ability to predict and counteract new attack strategies. For instance, machine learning can enhance the accuracy of threat detection systems by distinguishing between genuine and deceptive activities, thereby reducing false positives and improving the overall efficiency of cybersecurity measures. Additionally, machine learning algorithms can provide valuable insights into attacker behavior and tactics, informing the design of more effective deceptive measures.

Automation is another key trend that will influence the future of cybersecurity deception. The increasing complexity and scale of modern IT environments necessitate the automation of various aspects of deception strategy management. Automation allows for the efficient deployment, configuration, and orchestration of deceptive tools, reducing the manual effort required to maintain and operate these systems. Automated workflows can facilitate the rapid adjustment of deceptive tactics in response to real-time threat intelligence, ensuring that defenses remain agile and up-to-date. For example, automated scripts can deploy and manage multiple honeypots and decoys simultaneously, ensuring comprehensive coverage across diverse attack vectors. This scalability is essential for addressing the growing volume and complexity of cyber threats.

Furthermore, automation enables the seamless integration of deception with other security measures, such as threat intelligence platforms and incident response systems. By automating the collection and analysis of deception-related data, organizations can gain timely and actionable insights into attacker behavior and tactics. This integration enhances the overall effectiveness of cybersecurity strategies by providing a more comprehensive view of the threat landscape and enabling more informed decision-making.

Looking ahead, the intersection of cybersecurity deception with emerging technologies such as quantum computing presents both opportunities and challenges. Quantum computing has the potential to disrupt traditional encryption methods and significantly enhance computational power. This could impact the effectiveness of current deceptive techniques and necessitate the development of new approaches to counter quantum-enabled attacks. For example, quantum-resistant encryption algorithms and quantum-based deception technologies may become essential components of future cybersecurity strategies. Additionally, the advent of quantum computing could enable more advanced simulations and analysis, further enhancing the capabilities of deception tools.

Ethical considerations and regulatory compliance will also play a crucial role in shaping the future of cybersecurity deception. As deceptive techniques become more advanced and pervasive, it is essential to address concerns related to privacy, data protection, and the potential for unintended consequences. Organizations must develop clear guidelines and best practices for the ethical use of deception, ensuring that these measures are deployed responsibly and transparently. This includes addressing issues such as the potential impact on legitimate users, the handling of sensitive data, and the alignment of deception practices with legal and regulatory requirements.

In conclusion, the future of cybersecurity deception will be defined by the integration of AI, machine learning, and automation, which will enhance the sophistication and effectiveness of deceptive strategies. These technologies will enable the creation of highly realistic and adaptive deception tools, improve threat detection and response capabilities, and streamline the management of deceptive measures. The emergence of quantum computing and the need for ethical and regulatory considerations will also shape the direction of deception in cybersecurity. By staying informed about these trends and actively engaging with technological advancements, cybersecurity professionals can effectively navigate the evolving landscape and leverage deception to address new challenges and opportunities.

Integrating Deception with Other Security Strategies

In the dynamic landscape of cybersecurity, the integration of deception with traditional security measures is crucial for establishing a robust and multi-layered defense posture. To effectively harness the benefits of deception, it is essential to understand how it can complement and enhance existing security strategies, such as firewalls, intrusion detection systems (IDS), and encryption. This holistic approach ensures a more resilient defense against sophisticated threats, providing a comprehensive shield that addresses both known and emerging attack vectors.

Deception technologies, when integrated with firewalls, offer a powerful augmentation of network perimeter defenses. Firewalls serve as the first line of defense by filtering incoming and outgoing traffic based on predetermined security rules. While they are effective at blocking unauthorized access and mitigating known threats, they may not always detect advanced or novel attack methods. By incorporating deception technologies into the network environment, organizations can create a deceptive perimeter that lures attackers into engaging with decoy systems. These decoys can be designed to mimic critical infrastructure, such as servers or databases, which entices adversaries into interacting with controlled environments rather than genuine assets. This diversion not only improves the detection of malicious activities but also enhances the firewall's ability to identify and block attack attempts, as deceptive interactions can trigger alerts and provide valuable intelligence for fine-tuning firewall rules.

Intrusion detection systems (IDS) are another key component of a comprehensive security strategy. IDS monitor network traffic and system activities to identify suspicious behavior and potential breaches. The integration of deception with IDS can significantly enhance threat detection capabilities by enriching the data available for analysis. Deception tools, such as honeypots and trap systems, generate realistic traffic and interactions that mimic genuine activities. When an IDS encounters these deceptive elements, it can analyze them alongside legitimate traffic patterns to identify anomalies and potential threats. This enriched dataset allows the IDS to distinguish between benign and malicious activities more effectively, reducing false positives and increasing the accuracy of threat detection. Furthermore, the insights gained from deceptive interactions can inform the refinement of IDS rules and detection algorithms, improving overall system performance.

Encryption remains a cornerstone of data security, protecting sensitive information from unauthorized access. While encryption secures data at rest and in transit, it does not directly address the challenges of detecting and responding to cyber threats. Integrating deception with encryption strategies provides an additional layer of defense by enhancing the ability to detect and mitigate attacks targeting encrypted data. For instance, deceptive techniques can be employed to create fake encryption keys or deploy decoy encrypted files, which can trap and expose attackers attempting to access or manipulate sensitive data. This approach not only aids in identifying potential breaches but also provides actionable intelligence on the methods and tools used by adversaries to bypass encryption defenses. By combining deception with encryption, organizations can strengthen their overall security posture and improve their ability to safeguard critical information.

A holistic security approach also involves integrating deception with endpoint protection measures. Endpoint security solutions, such as antivirus software and endpoint detection and response (EDR) systems, focus on safeguarding individual devices from malware and other threats. Deception technologies can enhance endpoint protection by creating deceptive endpoints that attract and capture malicious activities targeting devices. These deceptive endpoints can be designed to appear as legitimate systems, drawing attackers away from genuine endpoints and allowing security teams to monitor and analyze their tactics. The data gathered from these deceptive interactions can inform the development of more effective endpoint protection strategies, including the detection of advanced persistent threats (APTs) and other sophisticated attack methods.

The integration of deception with security information and event management (SIEM) systems represents another critical aspect of a comprehensive security strategy. SIEM systems aggregate and analyze security event data from across the organization to provide a centralized view of the threat landscape. By incorporating deception data into SIEM platforms, organizations can gain a more detailed and nuanced understanding of potential threats. Deception technologies generate a wealth of information about attacker behavior, tactics, and techniques, which can be correlated with other security event data to identify patterns and detect emerging threats. This integration allows for more effective threat hunting, incident response, and forensic analysis, as security teams can leverage deception insights to enhance their overall security operations.

In conclusion, integrating deception with traditional security strategies is essential for building a robust and multi-layered defense framework. By augmenting firewalls, intrusion detection systems, encryption, endpoint protection measures, and SIEM platforms with deception technologies, organizations can create a more resilient security posture that addresses both known and emerging threats. This holistic approach not only improves threat detection and response capabilities but also enhances overall protection by leveraging the synergy between deceptive and traditional defensive layers. As the threat landscape continues to evolve, the strategic integration of deception with other security measures will remain a critical component of effective cybersecurity.

In integrating deception with other cybersecurity strategies, it is essential to consider how deception technologies can enhance and complement existing defenses, such as firewalls, intrusion detection systems, and encryption. This comprehensive approach not only strengthens the overall security posture but also ensures a more nuanced and adaptive defense mechanism.

To begin with, the integration of deception into network segmentation strategies can significantly bolster network security. Network segmentation divides the network into smaller, isolated segments to limit the spread of threats and confine malicious activities. By incorporating deceptive elements within these segments, organizations can create a more complex and confusing environment for attackers. For instance, deploying honeypots and decoy systems in various segments can mislead attackers into engaging with these deceptive components rather than real, sensitive systems. This diversion not only enhances threat detection but also allows for more precise identification of attack methods and potential vulnerabilities within each segment. The insights gained from these deceptive interactions can inform the refinement of segmentation rules and improve the overall effectiveness of the network security strategy.

Furthermore, the synergy between deception and threat intelligence can provide a more comprehensive understanding of the threat landscape. Threat intelligence platforms aggregate and analyze data about emerging threats, attack patterns, and adversary tactics. Integrating deception data into these platforms allows for a richer and more contextualized view of potential threats. For example, deception technologies can generate detailed information about attacker behavior, tactics, and tools, which can be used to enhance threat intelligence feeds. By correlating this deceptive data with other threat intelligence sources, organizations can gain deeper insights into attack trends and adjust their defensive measures accordingly. This integration helps in creating a more proactive and informed approach to threat detection and response.

Another critical aspect of integrating deception is its role in incident response and management. Incident response teams rely on various tools and techniques to detect, analyze, and respond to security incidents. Deception technologies can provide valuable intelligence during an incident by offering insights into attacker movements, tactics, and objectives. For instance, when an attacker interacts with a deceptive asset, the resulting data can be analyzed to understand the attacker's methods and intentions. This information can then be used to refine incident response strategies, enhance forensic investigations, and improve overall response effectiveness. Additionally, deceptive techniques can be employed to mislead and slow down attackers, giving incident response teams more time to contain and mitigate the threat.

The integration of deception with vulnerability management also plays a crucial role in strengthening security defenses.

Vulnerability management involves identifying, assessing, and addressing vulnerabilities within the system to prevent potential exploits. Deception technologies can aid in this process by providing insights into how attackers might exploit specific vulnerabilities. For example, deploying deceptive assets that mimic real systems can reveal how attackers target and exploit vulnerabilities, allowing organizations to address these weaknesses more effectively. By understanding the tactics used by adversaries in deceptive scenarios, organizations can prioritize vulnerability remediation efforts and improve their overall security posture.

Moreover, the combination of deception and security awareness training can enhance organizational resilience against social engineering attacks. Security awareness training educates employees about recognizing and responding to phishing attempts, scams, and other social engineering tactics. Integrating deceptive elements, such as simulated phishing campaigns or fake social engineering scenarios, into training programs can provide a more realistic and engaging learning experience. This approach helps employees recognize and respond to real-world threats more effectively, reducing the likelihood of successful social engineering attacks and improving overall security awareness.

Finally, the integration of deception with continuous monitoring and analytics systems is essential for maintaining an adaptive and proactive security posture. Continuous monitoring involves the real-time analysis of network traffic, system activities, and security events to detect potential threats. By incorporating deception data into monitoring and analytics platforms, organizations can gain a more comprehensive view of their security environment. For instance, monitoring deceptive interactions can provide early warning signs of potential attacks and help identify new threat patterns. This integration enhances the ability to detect and respond to emerging threats in a timely manner, ensuring that the security strategy remains effective and relevant.

In conclusion, integrating deception with traditional security strategies requires a thoughtful and strategic approach. By combining deception technologies with network segmentation, threat intelligence, incident response, vulnerability management, security awareness training, and continuous monitoring, organizations can create a more resilient and adaptive security framework. This holistic approach not only strengthens existing defenses but also provides a more nuanced understanding of potential threats and enhances overall protection. As the threat landscape continues to evolve, the effective integration of deception with other security measures will be crucial for maintaining a robust and comprehensive defense posture.

Integrating deception with other security strategies necessitates a comprehensive understanding of how different security technologies and practices can work synergistically to create a more robust defense framework. By embedding deception into various layers of cybersecurity, organizations can enhance their ability to detect, respond to, and mitigate threats more effectively.

One critical area where deception can significantly augment existing security measures is in the realm of intrusion detection systems (IDS). Traditional IDS technologies are designed to identify and alert on suspicious activities or anomalies based on known attack signatures or behavior patterns. However, these systems may not always recognize novel or sophisticated attack methods. By integrating deception into IDS frameworks, organizations can create dynamic and deceptive environments that actively lure attackers into engaging with fake assets. These deceptive elements can generate real-time alerts and detailed intelligence on attacker behavior, which can then be used to refine IDS rules and improve detection accuracy. For instance, deceptive decoys can be strategically placed within network traffic flows to attract malicious actors and trigger IDS alerts, thereby enhancing the system's ability to identify and respond to threats.

Another key integration point is with firewalls, which are fundamental in controlling and monitoring network traffic based on predefined security rules. While firewalls are effective at blocking unauthorized access and filtering traffic, they may not always provide visibility into sophisticated threats that bypass traditional security controls. Incorporating deception technologies can augment firewall defenses by creating deceptive zones or endpoints that attract and engage attackers. By monitoring interactions with these deceptive components, organizations can gain insights into attack vectors, tools, and techniques that might otherwise go undetected. This additional layer of intelligence can help in fine-tuning firewall rules and improving overall network segmentation strategies.

Encryption is another crucial aspect of cybersecurity that benefits from integration with deception strategies. Encryption ensures the confidentiality and integrity of data by encoding it so that only authorized parties can access it. While encryption provides a strong defense against data breaches and unauthorized access, it does not address the full spectrum of attack methods. Deception technologies can complement encryption by creating fake data or misleading environments that divert attackers' attention away from real, encrypted assets. For example, by deploying deceptive data stores that appear to hold valuable information, organizations can mislead attackers and protect sensitive data from being targeted. This approach not only adds an extra layer of security but also helps in identifying potential attack methods and intentions.

The integration of deception with vulnerability management is also vital for enhancing overall security. Vulnerability management involves identifying, assessing, and mitigating security weaknesses within an organization's infrastructure. While traditional vulnerability management practices focus on patching and remediation, they may not always account for how vulnerabilities are exploited in real-world scenarios. Deception technologies can provide valuable insights into the exploitation of vulnerabilities by creating realistic attack scenarios and observing how attackers interact with them. This information can be used to prioritize vulnerability remediation efforts based on actual exploitation techniques and to develop more effective security measures.

Moreover, the fusion of deception with endpoint protection strategies offers another significant advantage. Endpoint protection focuses on securing individual devices and endpoints from threats such as malware, ransomware, and unauthorized access. Deception technologies can enhance endpoint protection by deploying deceptive endpoints that mimic real devices but are designed to detect and analyze malicious activities. By monitoring interactions with these deceptive endpoints, organizations can gain insights into attack methods, malware behavior, and potential weaknesses in endpoint defenses. This approach allows for a more proactive and informed response to endpoint threats, improving overall protection.

Furthermore, integrating deception with security information and event management (SIEM) systems can enhance an organization's ability to analyze and respond to security events. SIEM systems collect, aggregate, and analyze security data from various sources to provide a centralized view of security events and incidents. By incorporating deception data into SIEM platforms, organizations can enrich their security analytics with insights from deceptive interactions. This integration enables a more comprehensive analysis of potential threats and helps in identifying patterns and anomalies that may indicate an ongoing attack. Additionally, it allows for more effective correlation of events and more precise incident response.

Finally, the integration of deception with security awareness training is crucial for building a resilient organizational culture. Security awareness training aims to educate employees about recognizing and responding to cybersecurity threats, such as phishing and social engineering attacks. By incorporating deceptive elements into training programs, organizations can create realistic and engaging scenarios that help employees develop practical skills for identifying and mitigating threats. For example, simulated phishing attacks and mock social engineering attempts can provide employees with hands-on experience and reinforce best practices for recognizing and responding to real-world threats.

In summary, integrating deception with other security strategies involves creating a multifaceted approach that leverages the strengths of various security technologies and practices. By enhancing traditional security measures such as firewalls, intrusion detection systems, and encryption with deceptive elements, organizations can improve threat detection, response, and mitigation capabilities. Additionally, the synergy between deception and vulnerability management, endpoint protection, SIEM systems, and security awareness training contributes to a more robust and adaptive security framework. This holistic approach not only strengthens overall defenses but also provides valuable insights into potential threats and vulnerabilities, enabling organizations to stay ahead of evolving attack methods and maintain a resilient security posture.

Designing Deceptive Network Architectures

Creating deceptive network architectures involves an intricate blend of network design principles and deception strategies to craft environments that can mislead and detect potential intruders. A well-designed deceptive network not only enhances the overall security posture but also provides valuable intelligence on attacker behaviors and tactics. The process of designing such architectures requires a deep understanding of both network operations and the techniques used by malicious actors to exploit network vulnerabilities.

The initial step in designing a deceptive network architecture is to establish clear objectives for the deception strategy. This includes defining the types of threats the network aims to detect, the specific information to be protected, and the overall goals of the deceptive elements. For instance, a network might be designed to detect internal threats, such as insider attacks or unauthorized access attempts, or to attract external attackers targeting sensitive data. Understanding these objectives will guide the design of the network and ensure that the deceptive elements align with the organization's security needs.

One of the core components of a deceptive network architecture is the creation of fake network segments. These segments are designed to appear as legitimate parts of the network but are actually isolated and controlled environments meant to deceive and engage attackers. To design effective fake network segments, it is crucial to consider their placement within the network topology. They should be integrated in such a way that they blend seamlessly with real network segments, creating a realistic and convincing environment for potential intruders.

To achieve this, fake network segments can be configured to mimic the characteristics of actual network segments, including IP address ranges, domain names, and network services. This can involve deploying fake servers, databases, and applications that resemble those found in the legitimate network. Additionally, these segments should be designed to emulate real network traffic patterns and behaviors to enhance their believability. By doing so, attackers who interact with these deceptive elements are more likely to be diverted from targeting critical assets and instead engage with the fake components.

Misleading configurations play a significant role in the effectiveness of deceptive network architectures. This can include deploying decoy systems with vulnerable configurations that are intended to attract attackers. For example, creating systems with known vulnerabilities or misconfigured services can entice attackers to engage with these decoys, providing valuable insights into their tactics and techniques. These misleading configurations should be carefully designed to avoid creating actual security risks or vulnerabilities within the real network.

Another important aspect of designing deceptive network architectures is the implementation of dynamic and adaptive deception elements. This involves creating a network environment that can evolve and adapt in response to attacker activities. For example, deceptive network segments can be periodically reconfigured or updated to reflect changes in the legitimate network environment, making it more challenging for attackers to distinguish between real and fake components. Additionally, dynamic deception can involve the deployment of automated tools that generate fake alerts, responses, and interactions to further confuse and mislead attackers.

To ensure that deceptive network elements blend seamlessly with legitimate operations, it is essential to maintain a balance between deception and real network traffic. This involves carefully monitoring and analyzing network traffic to ensure that deceptive elements do not disrupt legitimate operations or trigger false positives. Advanced monitoring and analysis tools can be employed to track interactions with deceptive components and correlate them with real network activities. This helps in distinguishing between genuine security incidents and deceptive interactions, enabling more accurate and effective responses.

The integration of deception into network security operations also requires collaboration between different teams within an organization. Network architects, security analysts, and incident responders must work together to design, implement, and manage deceptive network architectures. This collaboration ensures that the deceptive elements are aligned with overall security goals and that the intelligence gathered from deceptive interactions is effectively utilized to enhance security measures and response strategies.

Finally, testing and validation are critical steps in the design process of deceptive network architectures. Before deploying the deceptive elements into a live environment, it is important to conduct thorough testing to ensure their effectiveness and to identify any potential issues. This can involve simulating various attack scenarios to evaluate how well the deceptive elements attract and engage attackers, and to assess their impact on overall network performance and security. Continuous validation and refinement of the deceptive network components are necessary to maintain their effectiveness and to adapt to evolving threat landscapes.

In summary, designing deceptive network architectures involves a careful balance of creating realistic and convincing fake network segments, implementing misleading configurations, and integrating dynamic deception elements. By aligning the design with specific security objectives and maintaining seamless integration with legitimate network operations, organizations can enhance their ability to detect and respond to potential threats. Collaboration between different security teams and thorough testing and validation are essential to ensure the effectiveness and resilience of the deceptive network architecture.

Designing deceptive network architectures involves an intricate process where the goal is to create an environment that lures, detects, and misleads potential intruders while preserving the functionality and integrity of the genuine network. This nuanced approach necessitates a deep understanding of both network design and deception techniques, ensuring that deceptive elements effectively integrate with legitimate network operations.

To begin, it's essential to establish the context within which deception is employed. This involves identifying specific threats and objectives that the deception strategy aims to address. For instance, a network designed to detect insider threats might employ different deceptive techniques compared to a network intended to fend off external attackers. Understanding the threat landscape and organizational goals guides the design of deceptive network architectures, ensuring that they align with broader security objectives.

One of the foundational elements of a deceptive network is the creation of fake network segments. These segments should be crafted to appear as plausible and integral parts of the network while serving the purpose of deception. The design of these segments involves more than simply setting up fake servers or applications. It requires a thoughtful approach to mimic real network behavior accurately. This includes configuring IP address ranges, domain names, and network services to mirror those found in genuine segments. The objective is to create an environment that appears authentic to anyone who interacts with it, thereby increasing the likelihood of engaging potential attackers.

Fake network segments are most effective when they are strategically placed within the network topology. Their placement should be such that they blend seamlessly with the real network, avoiding any obvious discrepancies that might alert attackers to their deceptive nature. This requires a careful analysis of the network's structure and the typical paths that attackers might take. For example, deploying fake segments in areas where sensitive data or critical systems are typically located can increase the chances of attracting attackers who are targeting valuable assets.

Misleading configurations also play a crucial role in

the effectiveness of deceptive network architectures. These configurations are designed to attract and engage attackers by presenting enticing, yet false, opportunities. For instance, creating decoy systems with known vulnerabilities or misconfigured services can lure attackers into interacting with these deceptive elements. The key is to ensure that these configurations do not inadvertently create real vulnerabilities within the network. This involves rigorous testing and validation to verify that the deceptive elements achieve their intended purpose without compromising overall network security.

To maximize the effectiveness of deceptive network architectures, it is important to incorporate dynamic elements that can adapt to changing threat landscapes. Static deceptive elements may become predictable over time, reducing their effectiveness. Dynamic deception involves regularly updating and reconfiguring the deceptive components to reflect changes in the legitimate network environment. This could include altering the appearance of fake network segments, modifying misleading configurations, or introducing new deceptive elements. By maintaining a dynamic and evolving deceptive environment, organizations can keep attackers off balance and increase the likelihood of detecting and responding to their activities.

Another critical aspect of designing deceptive network architectures is the integration of monitoring and response mechanisms. It is not enough to deploy deceptive elements; organizations must also have systems in place to monitor interactions with these elements and respond effectively. This involves deploying monitoring tools that can capture and analyze interactions with deceptive components, such as network traffic and system logs. These tools should be capable of distinguishing between legitimate activities and those involving deceptive elements, providing insights into attacker behavior and tactics.

Effective response mechanisms are also essential. When an attacker interacts with a deceptive element, the organization should have procedures in place to investigate and respond to these interactions. This might involve isolating the deceptive element, analyzing the attacker's actions, and adjusting the deception strategy as needed. The insights gained from these interactions can be invaluable for refining security measures and improving the overall defense posture.

In addition to monitoring and response, it is crucial to ensure that deceptive network elements do not disrupt legitimate operations. This requires careful planning and implementation to avoid any negative impact on real network activities. For example, network traffic generated by deceptive elements should be carefully managed to prevent it from overwhelming or confusing legitimate traffic. Additionally, deceptive configurations should be designed to avoid any unintended consequences that could affect real systems or services.

Testing and validation are essential throughout the design and implementation process. Before deploying deceptive elements into a live environment, they should be thoroughly tested to ensure they function as intended and do not introduce any vulnerabilities or performance issues. This involves simulating various attack scenarios and analyzing how the deceptive elements perform under different conditions. Continuous testing and refinement are necessary to maintain the effectiveness of the deceptive network architecture and to adapt to evolving threat landscapes.

In conclusion, designing deceptive network architectures requires a meticulous approach that balances realism with security. By creating fake network segments, implementing misleading configurations, and incorporating dynamic and adaptive elements, organizations can build an environment that effectively attracts and engages attackers. Integrating monitoring and response mechanisms ensures that interactions with deceptive components are analyzed and addressed, while rigorous testing and validation help maintain the integrity and effectiveness of the deceptive network. This comprehensive approach not only enhances the organization's ability to detect and respond to threats but also contributes to a more robust and resilient security posture.

When advancing the design of deceptive network architectures, it is crucial to address the integration of these deceptive elements with existing network infrastructure and security protocols. This integration must be executed meticulously to ensure that deceptive practices do not disrupt legitimate operations or create unforeseen vulnerabilities.

One key aspect of this integration involves ensuring that deceptive elements are invisible to legitimate network users and systems. This necessitates a strategic placement of deceptive network components so they do not interfere with real network traffic or services. For example, deploying decoy servers and fake data repositories should be done in such a way that they do not cause unnecessary network congestion or present performance issues. The placement of these components must be well-considered, mimicking the layout of genuine network services to avoid detection and reduce the risk of accidental exposure.

Moreover, deceptive network elements must be designed to blend with real components seamlessly. This blending requires a high level of detail in replicating the appearance and behavior of real network components. For instance, fake network segments should be configured to mimic the operational characteristics of their genuine counterparts, including network traffic patterns, response times, and data formats. This attention to detail helps ensure that attackers cannot easily distinguish between deceptive and real network elements, thereby increasing the likelihood of engaging them.

An additional consideration is the interaction between deceptive network elements and existing security measures. For example, if a network is protected by an intrusion detection system (IDS) or a security information and event management (SIEM) system, it is essential that deceptive elements are incorporated into these systems' monitoring frameworks. This ensures that interactions with deceptive elements are logged and analyzed in the same way as interactions with real network components. Integrating deceptive elements with IDS or SIEM systems allows for a comprehensive view of network activity, including potential attacker behavior and patterns.

The deployment of deceptive network elements also involves careful coordination with other security controls, such as firewalls and encryption. Firewalls must be configured to allow traffic to and from deceptive elements without exposing them to unnecessary risk. Encryption practices should be uniformly applied to deceptive and legitimate traffic to prevent attackers from distinguishing between the two based on data encryption levels. Maintaining consistency in security controls across all network elements, both deceptive and real, is vital for creating a cohesive and effective security posture.

Furthermore, regular updates and maintenance are necessary to ensure the continued effectiveness of deceptive network architectures. As attackers evolve their techniques and tools, so too must the deceptive elements within the network. This involves periodically reviewing and updating deceptive components to reflect current threat trends and to adapt to changes in the legitimate network environment. Routine assessments and refinements help to maintain the relevancy and efficacy of the deception strategy, ensuring that it remains effective in detecting and misleading attackers.

Incorporating deception into network design also requires careful consideration of incident response and forensics. When an attacker engages with a deceptive element, it is crucial to have a clear process for investigating and analyzing the incident. This includes identifying and isolating the deceptive component involved, examining logs and data associated with the interaction, and assessing the attacker's methods and objectives. Insights gained from these investigations can be used to refine the deception strategy and enhance overall network security.

Effective communication and documentation are also essential throughout the design and implementation process. Clear documentation of the deceptive network architecture, including the placement and configuration of deceptive elements, helps ensure that all team members understand the structure and purpose of the deception strategy. This documentation serves as a reference for troubleshooting, maintenance, and future enhancements.

Training and awareness for network administrators and security personnel are also critical. These individuals must be well-versed in the design and operation of deceptive network components to manage them effectively and respond to any issues that may arise. Training programs should cover the objectives of the deception strategy, the functionality of deceptive elements, and the procedures for handling interactions with these elements.

In conclusion, designing deceptive network architectures requires a comprehensive and nuanced approach. Effective integration with existing infrastructure and security measures, attention to detail in replicating real network elements, and ongoing updates and maintenance are all critical factors in ensuring the success of the deception strategy. By carefully considering these elements, organizations can build robust deceptive network architectures that enhance their ability to detect and respond to threats while maintaining the integrity and functionality of legitimate network operations.

CHAPTER 21:

In examining the integration of deception with threat intelligence, it is essential to delve into the practical aspects of combining these elements to fortify an organization's security defenses. The synergy between deception techniques and threat intelligence is not merely a theoretical concept but a pragmatic approach to enhancing cybersecurity. This integration leverages the strengths of both disciplines to create a more dynamic and responsive security posture.

To begin with, the integration of deception with threat intelligence involves embedding deception strategies into the broader threat intelligence lifecycle. This means incorporating deceptive tactics into the initial stages of threat intelligence gathering, analysis, and dissemination. The deceptive elements, such as decoy systems, honeypots, and fake data repositories, serve as proactive tools to lure and engage adversaries. These elements are strategically placed within the network to mimic valuable assets or sensitive information, creating an environment where attackers are likely to interact with them.

The interactions that occur with these deceptive elements generate a wealth of data that can be analyzed to extract actionable threat intelligence. This data includes detailed information about attack vectors, exploitation techniques, and the tools used by the adversaries. By analyzing this data, security teams can gain insights into the tactics, techniques, and procedures employed by attackers. This analysis is crucial for understanding the evolving threat landscape and adapting defensive measures accordingly.

One significant advantage of integrating deception with threat intelligence is the ability to obtain early warnings of potential threats. Deceptive elements act as a detection mechanism, alerting security teams to suspicious activities before they reach critical assets. For example, if an attacker attempts to exploit a vulnerability in a deceptive system, this activity can be detected and investigated in real-time. The early detection of such activities provides security teams with valuable time to respond and mitigate the threat before it escalates.

The actionable intelligence gathered from deceptive interactions can be fed into threat intelligence platforms to enhance the organization's overall threat detection capabilities. Threat intelligence platforms aggregate data from various sources, including internal logs, external threat feeds, and deceptive elements. By integrating data from deceptive elements into these platforms, security teams can improve the accuracy and relevance of threat detection. This integration allows for a more comprehensive view of the threat landscape and enables the identification of patterns and trends that might otherwise go unnoticed.

Moreover, integrating deception with threat intelligence facilitates the identification of previously unknown threats. Deceptive elements often attract novel or sophisticated attackers who use advanced techniques to evade detection. The interactions with these elements can reveal new attack vectors, malware variants, or exploitation methods that are not yet widely known. This information is invaluable for updating threat intelligence databases and ensuring that detection mechanisms are equipped to handle emerging threats.

Another critical aspect of this integration is the correlation of deceptive data with other threat intelligence sources. The data collected from deceptive elements should be correlated with external threat feeds, internal security logs, and other intelligence sources to provide a comprehensive understanding of the threat environment. This correlation process involves analyzing data from different sources to identify patterns, validate threats, and refine detection strategies. By correlating deceptive data with other intelligence sources, security teams can enhance the accuracy of threat assessments and improve the effectiveness of their defensive measures.

The practical implementation of integrating deception with threat intelligence requires a well-defined strategy and clear objectives. Organizations should start by identifying the specific goals they aim to achieve through the integration. These goals may include improving threat detection, gaining insights into attacker behaviors, or identifying new threats. Once the objectives are established, security teams can design and deploy deceptive elements that align with these goals. This involves selecting the appropriate types of deception, such as honeypots or decoy systems, and configuring them to mimic legitimate assets or services.

In addition, organizations must ensure that their threat intelligence platforms are capable of ingesting and processing data from deceptive elements. This may involve configuring data feeds, integrating with SIEM systems, and establishing mechanisms for analyzing and correlating deceptive data. The integration process should be continuously monitored and refined to ensure that it remains effective in addressing evolving threats.

Case studies provide valuable insights into the effectiveness of integrating deception with threat intelligence. For instance, a financial institution that implemented deceptive data repositories reported significant improvements in threat detection and response. The deceptive repositories attracted cybercriminals attempting to steal sensitive information, and the data collected revealed new malware variants and attack techniques. This information was integrated into the institution's threat intelligence platform, enhancing its ability to detect and block similar threats.

Similarly, a technology company that deployed a network of honeypots to monitor cybercriminal activity gained valuable insights into the tactics used by attackers targeting its industry. The data collected from these honeypots was used to update the company's threat intelligence feeds, resulting in more accurate detection of sophisticated attacks and improved overall security.

In conclusion, integrating deception with threat intelligence offers a powerful approach to strengthening cybersecurity defenses. By leveraging deceptive techniques to gather actionable intelligence and incorporating this intelligence into threat detection and response strategies, organizations can gain a deeper understanding of attacker behaviors and improve their overall security posture. This integration requires careful planning, alignment with security objectives, and the use of advanced data collection and analysis tools to achieve the most effective outcomes.

Integrating deception with threat intelligence not only augments traditional security measures but also introduces a dynamic dimension to the threat management process. To fully exploit the potential of this integration, one must delve into the mechanisms by which deception tactics can be interwoven with threat intelligence systems and strategies.

In practical terms, integrating deception techniques involves embedding deceptive elements into existing threat intelligence frameworks. This integration enables security teams to create a more nuanced and responsive defense system. The deceptive elements, such as honeypots and decoy systems, function as advanced sensors within the network. They gather real-time data on attacker behaviors and tactics, providing valuable insights that traditional security tools might miss.

The first step in this integration process is to ensure that deceptive elements are strategically placed within the network. This requires a thorough understanding of the network architecture and potential attack vectors. Deceptive elements should be positioned in locations where attackers are likely to attempt unauthorized access or exploit vulnerabilities. For instance, placing honeypots in areas that mimic critical business operations can attract attackers who are probing for sensitive information. This placement not only increases the likelihood of engaging with potential threats but also ensures that the data collected is relevant to the organization's specific security context.

Once the deceptive elements are deployed, the next step is to integrate the data collected from these elements with the organization's threat intelligence systems. This involves configuring threat intelligence platforms to ingest and analyze data from the deceptive elements. The integration process may include setting up data pipelines that feed information from honeypots, decoy systems, and other deceptive tactics into threat intelligence databases. This ensures that the threat intelligence systems have a comprehensive view of the threat landscape, including insights gained from deceptive interactions.

Analyzing the data from deceptive elements involves several key processes. Initially, raw data collected from honeypots or decoys must be cleaned and normalized to ensure consistency and accuracy. This process includes filtering out irrelevant information and standardizing data formats. Once cleaned, the data is subjected to advanced analytical techniques to identify patterns, anomalies, and indicators of compromise. Machine learning algorithms and data analytics tools can enhance this process by automating the detection of suspicious activities and correlating data from different sources.

The integration of deception data with threat intelligence feeds enhances the organization's ability to detect and respond to sophisticated attacks. By combining insights from deceptive elements with external threat intelligence sources, such as threat feeds and industry reports, security teams can gain a more comprehensive understanding of emerging threats. This holistic view allows for the identification of trends and correlations that might otherwise go unnoticed. For example, if a particular malware variant is detected interacting with a honeypot, this information can be cross-referenced with external threat intelligence feeds to determine if the variant is part of a larger attack campaign or has been observed in other contexts.

Moreover, integrating deception with threat intelligence provides a mechanism for validating and refining security measures. The data collected from deceptive elements can be used to test the effectiveness of existing security controls and identify potential gaps. For instance, if an attacker successfully bypasses a decoy system, this could indicate a need for enhanced detection capabilities or a review of the current security posture. By continuously monitoring and analyzing deceptive interactions, security teams can make data-driven decisions to improve their defenses and address emerging threats.

Real-world examples illustrate the effectiveness of this integration. Consider a scenario where a financial institution deploys a network of honeypots to monitor for unauthorized access attempts. The data collected from these honeypots reveals patterns of behavior that suggest attackers are using advanced techniques to evade detection. By integrating this data with threat intelligence feeds, the institution identifies that these techniques are associated with a new type of attack targeting financial institutions. This information enables the institution to update its threat intelligence and adjust its security measures to better protect against the emerging threat.

Similarly, a technology company that uses deceptive data repositories to attract cybercriminals can leverage the insights gained from these interactions to enhance its threat intelligence capabilities. The data reveals new attack vectors and malware variants that were previously unknown. By integrating this information with existing threat intelligence sources, the company can improve its ability to detect and respond to similar attacks in the future. This proactive approach not only enhances the company's overall security posture but also contributes to the broader cybersecurity community by sharing newly discovered threats and vulnerabilities.

The integration of deception with threat intelligence is not without its challenges. Ensuring that deceptive elements are correctly configured and do not interfere with legitimate network operations is crucial. Additionally, managing the volume of data generated by deceptive elements and ensuring its relevance to threat intelligence efforts requires careful planning and resources. Organizations must also address potential privacy and legal considerations when deploying deceptive tactics, particularly when dealing with sensitive or personal information.

In conclusion, the integration of deception with threat intelligence represents a powerful approach to enhancing cybersecurity defenses. By embedding deceptive elements into threat intelligence frameworks and analyzing the data collected, organizations can gain valuable insights into attacker behaviors, improve threat detection capabilities, and refine their security measures. This integration provides a dynamic and responsive defense mechanism that complements traditional security measures and helps organizations stay ahead of evolving threats. The successful implementation of this integration requires careful planning, strategic deployment of deceptive elements, and continuous monitoring and analysis to ensure that it effectively enhances the overall security posture.

CHAPTER 22:

Designing custom deception solutions requires a nuanced understanding of both technical and organizational factors. After identifying specific needs and designing tailored tools, the focus shifts to the implementation phase. This phase is crucial as it ensures that the deception solutions are not only functional but also seamlessly integrate with existing security infrastructure, providing the intended benefits without disrupting normal operations.

The implementation of custom deception solutions begins with establishing a clear deployment strategy. This involves deciding where and how the deception tools will be integrated into the network. The deployment strategy should align with the overall security architecture and address the specific threats the organization faces. For example, if the primary concern is insider threats, the deployment might focus on creating deceptive environments within key internal systems. Conversely, for external threats, the focus might be on integrating deception mechanisms in perimeter defenses or within exposed network segments.

Once the deployment strategy is in place, the next step is to configure and deploy the deceptive elements. This process requires careful attention to detail to ensure that the deception tools are both effective and unobtrusive. Configuration involves setting up the deception tools with realistic parameters and ensuring that they mimic legitimate systems or data convincingly. For instance, if deploying a honeypot, it should be configured with authentic-looking files and services that would attract an attacker's attention. Similarly, decoy servers should be configured to resemble real servers in terms of network activity and responsiveness.

During deployment, it is crucial to maintain a balance between visibility and concealment. Deceptive elements need to be visible enough to attract attackers but not so conspicuous that they raise suspicion or become obvious targets. The challenge lies in ensuring that these deceptive elements blend seamlessly with the actual network infrastructure. This can be achieved by embedding them in such a way that they appear as natural parts of the environment, avoiding any configuration that might reveal their deceptive nature.

Another key aspect of implementing custom deception solutions is ensuring proper integration with existing security tools and processes. Deception tools should be connected to central logging and monitoring systems to facilitate real-time analysis and response. Integration with Security Information and Event Management (SIEM) systems allows for the aggregation and correlation of data from both deceptive and legitimate sources. This integration enhances the ability to detect and respond to threats by providing a more comprehensive view of network activity and potential intrusions.

The effectiveness of deception solutions is closely tied to their ongoing management and maintenance. After deployment, it is essential to regularly monitor and update the deceptive elements to ensure they continue to function as intended. This includes tracking the interactions with deceptive elements, analyzing patterns, and adjusting configurations as needed. For instance, if an attacker begins to avoid certain decoys, it may be necessary to update these elements or introduce new ones to maintain their effectiveness.

Maintenance also involves periodic reviews of the deception

strategy to ensure it remains aligned with the organization's evolving security needs. As threat landscapes and attack techniques change, the deception tools must be adapted to address new challenges. This ongoing evaluation helps to identify any gaps in the deception strategy and make necessary adjustments to enhance overall effectiveness.

In addition to technical considerations, it is important to address the organizational aspects of deploying custom deception solutions. This includes training personnel on the use and management of deception tools, as well as integrating deception into broader security policies and procedures. Security teams should be familiar with how to interpret data from deceptive elements and how to respond to alerts generated by these tools. Proper training ensures that the team can effectively leverage the deception solutions to enhance overall security posture.

Case studies of organizations that have successfully developed and implemented custom deception solutions provide valuable insights into best practices and lessons learned. For example, a healthcare organization facing challenges with protecting sensitive patient data implemented a custom deception solution involving fake patient records and deceptive access points within its electronic health record (EHR) system. This solution helped to detect and mitigate unauthorized access attempts while providing valuable insights into the methods used by potential attackers.

Another example is a technology company that developed a bespoke deception solution to address threats targeting its intellectual property. The company implemented decoy environments that replicated its research and development infrastructure. These decoy environments were designed to attract and engage attackers, providing early warnings of attempts to steal sensitive information. By analyzing interactions with these decoys, the company was able to refine its threat detection capabilities and better protect its valuable intellectual assets.

In summary, the development and implementation of custom deception solutions require a detailed and methodical approach. From identifying organizational needs and designing tailored tools to deploying and integrating these tools into the existing security infrastructure, each step is critical to achieving the desired outcomes. Effective management and ongoing maintenance ensure that deception solutions remain effective and responsive to emerging threats. By learning from successful case studies and applying best practices, organizations can develop custom deception solutions that significantly enhance their overall security posture.

In developing custom deception solutions, the final stage involves evaluating their effectiveness and making adjustments based on performance metrics and evolving organizational needs. This assessment is critical to ensuring that the deception tools provide the intended benefits and adapt to new threat landscapes.

To begin the evaluation process, I first conduct a comprehensive review of how the deception solutions are functioning within the live environment. This includes analyzing the interactions and data collected from the deceptive elements, such as honeypots, decoys, and misleading configurations. The goal is to determine whether these elements are effectively attracting and engaging potential attackers. Key performance indicators, such as the number and types of interactions, the sophistication of attacks, and the timeliness of detection, are analyzed to assess the overall impact of the deception tools.

A crucial aspect of this evaluation involves examining the quality and relevance of the intelligence gathered through the deceptive elements. I assess whether the data collected is actionable and provides meaningful insights into attacker behavior and tactics. This analysis helps in understanding whether the deception tools are effectively complementing other security measures and contributing to a more comprehensive defense strategy. If the intelligence gathered is lacking in detail or relevance, it may be necessary to refine the deceptive elements or adjust their deployment to improve their effectiveness.

In addition to evaluating the technical performance of the deception tools, I also consider their operational impact. This involves assessing whether the deception elements are causing any unintended disruptions or interference with legitimate network activities. For instance, if a decoy server is inadvertently receiving high volumes of traffic that affect its performance, adjustments may be required to balance the load and maintain the integrity of legitimate operations. Ensuring that the deception tools are seamlessly integrated into the existing infrastructure without disrupting normal operations is essential for their long-term success.

Continuous monitoring and analysis are integral to maintaining the effectiveness of custom deception solutions. I implement regular reviews and updates based on emerging threats, changes in the organizational environment, and feedback from security personnel. This proactive approach ensures that the deception tools remain relevant and responsive to evolving threat landscapes. It also allows for the identification and rectification of any weaknesses or gaps in the deception strategy.

Moreover, collaboration with other security teams and stakeholders is important in refining the deception solutions. Engaging with incident response teams, threat intelligence analysts, and network administrators provides valuable insights into how the deception tools are being utilized and how they can be improved. Regular discussions and feedback sessions help in aligning the deception strategy with broader security objectives and addressing any operational challenges that arise.

Case studies of organizations that have successfully developed custom deception solutions offer practical examples and lessons learned. One notable example is a financial institution that created a sophisticated deception environment to protect against advanced persistent threats (APTs). The organization deployed a network of decoy servers and fake financial systems designed to mimic its real infrastructure. By analyzing the interactions with these deceptive elements, the institution gained valuable insights into the tactics and techniques used by attackers targeting financial data. This information was used to enhance overall security measures and better protect against similar threats in the future.

Another example involves a multinational corporation that developed a custom deception solution to address insider threats. The corporation implemented deceptive elements within its internal network, including fake access points and misleading data repositories. These deception tools were designed to detect and analyze unauthorized access attempts by employees or contractors. The intelligence gathered through these tools provided insights into potential insider threats and helped the organization strengthen its internal security measures.

The development and implementation of custom deception solutions require a meticulous approach, combining technical expertise with strategic foresight. From the initial design and deployment to ongoing evaluation and refinement, each stage is crucial to achieving effective and resilient deception strategies. By carefully monitoring performance, integrating feedback, and learning from real-world applications, organizations can develop and maintain deception solutions that significantly enhance their overall security posture.

CHAPTER 23:

The development of a robust training and awareness program for deploying deception strategies is an ongoing process that requires continuous effort and adaptation. To ensure that the training remains relevant and effective, it is crucial to incorporate feedback mechanisms and iterative improvements. This process begins by establishing a feedback loop where participants can share their experiences and suggestions regarding the training. Gathering insights from those who have actively engaged with deception technologies allows for the identification of gaps and areas for enhancement. By analyzing feedback, organizations can refine training content, address emerging issues, and adapt to changes in the threat landscape or technological advancements.

Interactive and immersive training methods can greatly enhance the learning experience. For example, creating virtual environments or using simulation platforms allows security personnel to practice deploying and managing deception tools in a controlled setting. These environments replicate real-world scenarios where participants can interact with deceptive elements, observe attacker behavior, and refine their response strategies. The use of gamification techniques, where participants earn rewards or recognition for successful engagement with deception technologies, can further motivate and engage individuals in the training process. Such immersive experiences not only improve skill retention but also foster a deeper understanding of how deception strategies operate within a broader security framework.

Another critical aspect of training is the inclusion of cross-functional collaboration. Deception strategies often involve various teams and stakeholders within an organization, including IT, security operations, and incident response teams. Ensuring that all relevant departments are involved in the training process helps to foster a cohesive approach to deception deployment. Cross-functional training sessions can facilitate communication and coordination between teams, ensuring that everyone is aligned on objectives, responsibilities, and procedures. This collaborative approach also helps to address any potential gaps in knowledge or coordination that may arise during the deployment of deception strategies.

In addition to formal training programs, ongoing professional development opportunities are essential for keeping personnel up-to-date with the latest advancements in deception technologies and techniques. Encouraging team members to participate in industry conferences, webinars, and workshops provides exposure to cutting-edge research and emerging trends. Networking with other professionals in the field can offer valuable insights and best practices that can be incorporated into the organization's deception strategy. Furthermore, subscribing to relevant journals and publications ensures that the team remains informed about new developments and potential innovations in deception technology.

The effectiveness of deception strategies also hinges on the ability to adapt to evolving threats and tactics. Training programs should include components that address the dynamic nature of cyber threats and the continuous evolution of attacker techniques. By incorporating real-time threat intelligence and current threat trends into the training curriculum, personnel can better understand how deception strategies can be tailored to address new and emerging threats. This proactive approach ensures that deception tools remain relevant and effective in countering sophisticated adversaries.

Regular evaluation and assessment of the training program are vital for measuring its impact and effectiveness. This involves not only testing participants' knowledge and skills but also assessing how well they apply their training in real-world scenarios. Conducting periodic assessments and simulations can help identify any areas where additional training or support may be needed. Additionally, tracking metrics such as the success rate of detecting and engaging attackers, the efficiency of incident response, and overall security posture can provide valuable insights into the effectiveness of the deception strategy and its alignment with organizational goals.

In summary, establishing a comprehensive training and awareness program for deploying deception strategies requires a multifaceted approach that includes ongoing education, interactive training methods, cross-functional collaboration, and continuous improvement. By integrating feedback mechanisms, incorporating immersive training experiences, and staying informed about industry advancements, organizations can enhance their ability to effectively deploy and manage deception technologies. Ensuring that all relevant personnel are well-trained and aware of the purpose and application of deception tools is essential for maximizing their effectiveness and achieving a robust security posture.

The development and deployment of deception strategies are complex processes that require not only technical expertise but also an understanding of the organizational culture and human factors involved. To ensure the successful integration of deception technologies, it is essential to create a supportive environment that fosters awareness and competence among all relevant personnel. This involves addressing not only the technical aspects of deception but also the psychological and operational dimensions that influence how these strategies are perceived and implemented.

One of the critical factors in ensuring effective training is to align the objectives of the deception program with the broader security goals of the organization. This alignment helps to clarify the purpose of deception technologies and how they contribute to the overall security posture. It is vital to articulate the value of deception in a way that resonates with different stakeholders, including executive leadership, IT staff, and security analysts. By demonstrating how deception tools can enhance threat detection, reduce response times, and provide valuable intelligence, organizations can build a stronger case for their implementation and garner support from key decision-makers.

Furthermore, the creation of detailed training materials that address both the theoretical and practical aspects of deception is essential. These materials should include comprehensive explanations of how deception technologies work, the types of threats they are designed to address, and the best practices for their deployment and management. Visual aids, such as diagrams, flowcharts, and case studies, can enhance understanding and retention. Providing real-world examples and scenarios helps to contextualize the use of deception tools and illustrates their practical applications. This approach ensures that training participants not only grasp the technical details but also appreciate the strategic value of deception in various operational contexts.

Hands-on experience is a crucial component of effective training. Practical exercises that simulate real-world attack scenarios allow participants to apply their knowledge and skills in a controlled environment. These exercises should be designed to replicate the types of attacks that the organization is likely to encounter, using realistic data and systems. By engaging in these simulations, security teams can gain firsthand experience in deploying and managing deception technologies, identifying and responding to threats, and assessing the effectiveness of their strategies. These practical experiences also help to build confidence and competence, which are essential for the successful implementation of deception tactics in real-world situations.

Another important aspect of training is to address the potential challenges and pitfalls associated with deception technologies. Participants should be made aware of common issues such as the risk of false positives, the potential for attacker evasion, and the need for ongoing maintenance and updates. By understanding these challenges, security teams can develop strategies to mitigate risks and ensure that deception tools remain effective over time. Additionally, training should emphasize the importance of continuous learning and adaptation, as the threat landscape and attacker techniques are constantly evolving.

To reinforce the training and ensure that it translates into effective practice, regular follow-up sessions and refresher courses are necessary. These sessions provide opportunities to review and update training content, address any new developments or changes in the threat landscape, and reinforce key concepts and skills. Ongoing education helps to keep security personnel informed about the latest advancements in deception technologies and best practices, ensuring that their knowledge and skills remain current.

Building a culture of security awareness and collaboration is also crucial for the successful deployment of deception strategies. Encouraging open communication and collaboration between different teams, such as IT, security operations, and incident response, fosters a shared understanding of the goals and benefits of deception technologies. By working together and sharing insights and experiences, teams can develop a more cohesive and effective approach to deploying and managing deception tools.

Finally, it is essential to measure the effectiveness of the training program and make data-driven decisions for continuous improvement. This involves evaluating the impact of the training on participants' knowledge, skills, and performance, as well as assessing the overall effectiveness of the deception strategies in achieving their intended goals. Collecting and analyzing metrics such as the number of detected threats, response times, and incident outcomes provides valuable insights into the success of the training and the deployment of deception technologies.

In conclusion, the successful deployment of deception strategies relies on a comprehensive and well-structured training and awareness program. By aligning training objectives with organizational goals, creating detailed and practical training materials, providing hands-on experience, addressing potential challenges, and fostering a culture of collaboration and continuous improvement, organizations can ensure that their security teams are well-prepared to effectively utilize deception technologies. Through these efforts, deception can be integrated seamlessly into the broader security framework, enhancing overall protection and resilience against evolving cyber threats.

CHAPTER 24:

In further exploring the synergy between deception techniques and behavioral analytics, it is crucial to delve into how behavioral insights can refine and optimize the deployment of deceptive measures. Behavioral analytics provides a nuanced understanding of user interactions, allowing for the identification of deviations from normal behavior that may signal malicious intent. This depth of understanding can be harnessed to enhance the precision and relevance of deception strategies, ensuring that they are not only more effective but also more aligned with the specific threat landscape faced by an organization.

Behavioral analytics employs sophisticated algorithms to scrutinize data patterns and detect anomalies. These algorithms can identify subtle deviations in user behavior that might elude traditional security measures. For example, if a user suddenly begins accessing files they have never interacted with before, or if there is an unusual surge in network traffic, these patterns could indicate an insider threat or a compromised account. By integrating these insights into a deception framework, organizations can create more targeted and contextually relevant deceptive assets.

One effective approach is to use behavioral analytics to dynamically adjust the characteristics of deceptive environments. For instance, if the analytics reveal that an attacker is focusing on certain types of data or systems, deception tools can be reconfigured to simulate the presence of these specific assets. This adaptability ensures that deceptive measures remain relevant and capable of engaging attackers in a manner that reflects their evolving tactics. The ability to dynamically adjust deception based on behavioral data can lead to more successful identification and mitigation of threats.

Additionally, behavioral analytics can enhance the strategic placement of deception elements within a network. Traditional deception might involve placing decoys or honeypots in predictable locations. However, with insights gained from behavioral analytics, organizations can place these elements more strategically based on observed attack vectors and user behavior. For instance, if analytics suggest that attackers are likely to target specific areas of the network, deception elements can be placed in those areas to increase the likelihood of detection. This strategic placement not only improves the efficiency of deception but also reduces the risk of attackers bypassing these traps.

The integration of behavioral analytics also supports a more refined approach to handling false positives. Deception strategies can sometimes generate false alarms, where legitimate activities are mistakenly flagged as malicious. Behavioral analytics can help mitigate this issue by providing a more detailed context for observed activities. By analyzing patterns and correlating behaviors with known attack signatures, behavioral analytics can help distinguish between benign and suspicious activities more accurately. This improved accuracy reduces the likelihood of unnecessary alerts and allows security teams to focus on genuine threats.

Moreover, the combination of behavioral analytics and deception facilitates a deeper understanding of attacker methodologies. Analyzing how attackers interact with deceptive elements can yield valuable insights into their techniques, tools, and objectives. For instance, if an attacker consistently bypasses certain types of deception or manipulates them in specific ways, this information can be used to adjust the deception strategy accordingly. Such insights contribute to a more comprehensive understanding of attacker behavior, which can inform future security measures and improve overall defense mechanisms.

The practical application of integrating behavioral analytics with deception can be observed in various real-world scenarios. In a retail environment, for example, behavioral analytics might reveal unusual patterns in transaction data that suggest fraudulent activity. By deploying deceptive elements such as fake transaction records or misleading product listings, the organization can attract and identify the perpetrators. The insights gained from behavioral analytics allow for the continuous refinement of these deceptive tactics, ensuring that they remain effective against evolving threats.

Similarly, in a corporate setting, behavioral analytics can be used to monitor employee activities and detect deviations that may indicate insider threats. Deceptive measures, such as creating fake internal communication channels or false project information, can be employed to identify malicious insiders. The integration of behavioral data helps to fine-tune these deceptive elements, making them more effective in detecting and addressing potential threats.

In summary, the synergy between behavioral analytics and deception techniques offers a powerful approach to enhancing cybersecurity. By leveraging behavioral insights to inform and refine deception strategies, organizations can create more adaptive, precise, and effective security measures. This integration not only improves the ability to detect and mitigate threats but also contributes to a deeper understanding of attacker behaviors and methodologies. As the threat landscape continues to evolve, the combination of behavioral analytics and deception provides a dynamic and responsive approach to safeguarding digital environments.

In the realm of cybersecurity, integrating deception techniques with behavioral analytics represents a pivotal advancement in enhancing defense mechanisms. To further elucidate this synergy, it is crucial to understand the practical implications and methodologies for combining these strategies effectively. Behavioral analytics, through its detailed examination of user activities and patterns, provides a robust foundation for refining deception tactics, thereby increasing their impact and utility in threat detection.

One of the key benefits of combining deception with behavioral analytics is the ability to create highly customized and responsive deceptive environments. Behavioral analytics allows for real-time monitoring of network and user activities, which can then be used to adapt and evolve deception tactics based on observed behaviors. For instance, if analytics reveal a significant amount of lateral movement within a network, deception strategies can be adjusted to create additional fake assets or mislead attackers into engaging with decoys that mimic the structures and behaviors of critical systems. This level of customization ensures that deception measures are not static but are dynamically aligned with the threat landscape, thereby enhancing their effectiveness.

Furthermore, the integration of behavioral analytics facilitates a more nuanced approach to threat prioritization. By analyzing patterns and anomalies, organizations can identify which deceptive elements are most likely to engage attackers based on their behaviors. This enables the prioritization of certain deceptive assets over others, ensuring that resources are allocated effectively and that the most critical areas of the network are protected. For example, if analytics indicate that an attacker is targeting specific types of data or systems, deception strategies can be tailored to focus on these areas, increasing the likelihood of detecting and mitigating the threat.

In addition to enhancing the specificity and relevance of deceptive measures, behavioral analytics also aids in refining the effectiveness of deception through improved response mechanisms. When deceptive elements are triggered, behavioral data can provide immediate feedback on how attackers interact with these elements. This feedback loop is invaluable for adjusting the deception strategy in real time. For instance, if an attacker bypasses a particular deceptive layer or manipulates it in an unexpected way, behavioral analytics can identify these deviations, allowing security teams to rapidly adapt their tactics to address the new methods employed by the attacker. This dynamic response capability ensures that deception measures remain effective even as attackers evolve their strategies.

Moreover, behavioral analytics contributes significantly to the reduction of false positives in deceptive environments. Traditional deception strategies might generate numerous alerts, some of which may be false positives or benign activities mistakenly flagged as suspicious. By leveraging behavioral analytics, organizations can gain a deeper understanding of normal user behaviors and their variations, which helps to distinguish between legitimate and malicious activities more accurately. For instance, analytics can provide context for unusual patterns by correlating them with historical data and known threat indicators, thereby reducing the likelihood of unnecessary alerts and allowing security teams to focus on genuine threats.

The practical application of this integration can be observed through various case studies. In financial institutions, where the protection of sensitive data is paramount, combining deception with behavioral analytics has proven effective in identifying and mitigating advanced threats. For example, when behavioral analytics reveal unusual access patterns or unauthorized attempts to interact with critical financial records, deceptive measures such as fake transaction records or simulated financial systems can be employed to engage the attackers. The behavioral data collected from these interactions can then be analyzed to refine the deception strategy and improve the overall security posture.

Similarly, in a corporate setting, where insider threats pose a significant risk, the integration of behavioral analytics and deception helps in monitoring and detecting malicious insider activities. By analyzing employee behavior and identifying anomalies, organizations can deploy deceptive elements such as false internal communications or fabricated project details to uncover potential threats. The insights gained from behavioral analytics allow for a more tailored and responsive approach to managing these deceptive elements, ensuring that they are effective in detecting and mitigating insider threats.

In conclusion, the fusion of deception techniques with behavioral analytics offers a sophisticated and adaptive approach to cybersecurity. By leveraging behavioral insights to inform and refine deception strategies, organizations can enhance their ability to detect and address threats more effectively. This integration not only improves the precision and relevance of deceptive measures but also contributes to a deeper understanding of attacker behaviors and methodologies. As the cybersecurity landscape continues to evolve, the combination of deception and behavioral analytics provides a dynamic and responsive defense mechanism, ensuring that organizations are better equipped to safeguard their digital environments against emerging threats.

CHAPTER 25:

A multinational technology firm specializing in cloud computing and data storage faced a growing threat from cybercriminals targeting their extensive network of cloud services. Recognizing the need for a more nuanced approach to security, the firm opted to integrate deception technology into its defenses. The firm's objective was to enhance its ability to detect and mitigate advanced persistent threats (APTs) and insider attacks.

To achieve this, the firm developed a sophisticated deception framework that included deploying decoy cloud instances and simulated data storage environments. These deceptive elements were meticulously designed to mirror the firm's actual cloud infrastructure and data storage systems. One of the primary challenges was ensuring that these decoys did not disrupt the operation of the legitimate cloud services while maintaining a high degree of realism to attract potential attackers.

A significant hurdle was integrating the deception technology with the firm's existing cloud management platforms and security operations. The firm's IT and security teams had to collaborate closely to design and deploy the decoy instances without affecting the performance of the genuine cloud services. Additionally, the integration required configuring the firm's cloud management tools to recognize and handle alerts generated by the deceptive elements.

The results of this deception implementation were markedly positive. The decoy cloud instances successfully attracted several APT groups, providing the firm with critical insights into the tactics and techniques employed by these sophisticated attackers. By analyzing the interactions with the deceptive environments, the firm was able to identify patterns indicative of advanced threats and refine its defensive measures accordingly. The implementation also resulted in a notable reduction in the time taken to detect and respond to potential security incidents, enhancing the firm's overall threat management capabilities.

In the retail sector, a major e-commerce company faced increasing security challenges related to protecting customer data and preventing fraud. The company decided to deploy a deception strategy aimed at detecting and mitigating fraudulent activities, such as account takeovers and payment fraud. This involved the creation of fake user accounts and fraudulent transaction scenarios designed to lure attackers and gather actionable intelligence.

One of the main challenges was ensuring that the deceptive elements were indistinguishable from legitimate accounts and transactions. The company's security team needed to develop convincing fake profiles and transactions that would attract attackers without arousing suspicion among legitimate users. Additionally, the integration of the deception technology with the company's existing fraud detection systems required careful planning to ensure that alerts from the deceptive elements were accurately categorized and prioritized.

The results of the deception strategy were substantial. The fake user accounts and transaction scenarios successfully attracted several fraud attempts, allowing the company to identify and block fraudulent activities before they could impact genuine accounts. The insights gained from analyzing these interactions helped the company enhance its fraud detection algorithms and improve its overall security posture. The implementation of deception technology also contributed to a reduction in false positives, as the system became more adept at distinguishing between genuine and deceptive activities.

In the energy sector, a large utility company sought to strengthen its defenses against cyber threats targeting its critical infrastructure. The company implemented a deception strategy involving the deployment of fake control systems and simulated operational data designed to attract and engage potential attackers targeting its energy grid. The goal was to enhance the detection of attacks and gather intelligence on adversaries' tactics and techniques.

One of the primary challenges was ensuring that the deceptive control systems and data simulations accurately reflected the real operational environment without introducing vulnerabilities. The utility company's security team had to work closely with operational technology experts to design and deploy the decoy systems in a way that would not interfere with legitimate operations or compromise the integrity of the actual control systems.

The deception strategy proved highly effective in detecting and mitigating cyber threats. The fake control systems attracted several sophisticated attack attempts, providing valuable insights into the methods used by adversaries targeting critical infrastructure. The analysis of these interactions allowed the company to enhance its defensive measures and improve its overall threat detection capabilities. Additionally, the implementation of deception technology helped the utility company build a more resilient security posture, capable of withstanding and responding to advanced threats.

Each of these case studies illustrates the practical application of deception technology in diverse industry contexts. The challenges faced ranged from integrating deceptive elements with existing systems to ensuring the realism of the decoys. However, the successful implementation of these strategies demonstrated the value of deception in enhancing threat detection and improving overall security posture. By learning from these real-world examples, organizations can gain valuable insights into the effective deployment of deception strategies and apply these lessons to strengthen their own security practices.

In the financial sector, a global bank sought to address the increasing sophistication of cyber attacks targeting its sensitive data and transaction systems. The bank's approach involved the deployment of deception technology to protect its high-value assets, including transaction processing systems and customer data repositories. The primary objective was to detect and counteract malicious activities by creating a network of fake financial systems and decoy data that would attract and engage potential attackers.

The implementation of this deception strategy presented several challenges. One of the key issues was ensuring that the deceptive financial systems appeared genuine and seamlessly integrated into the bank's existing infrastructure. The bank's IT and security teams had to develop sophisticated fake transaction systems and data repositories that mimicked the bank's real assets without introducing vulnerabilities or impacting legitimate operations. Additionally, integrating these deceptive elements with the bank's security monitoring and incident response systems required careful coordination to ensure that alerts from the deceptive environments were properly analyzed and acted upon.

Despite these challenges, the deception strategy yielded impressive results. The fake financial systems successfully attracted several targeted attacks, providing the bank with valuable insights into the tactics and techniques used by sophisticated cybercriminals. By analyzing these interactions, the bank was able to identify new attack vectors and refine its defensive measures. The implementation of deception technology also led to an improvement in the bank's overall threat detection capabilities, allowing it to more effectively identify and respond to potential security incidents.

A healthcare organization faced the daunting task of protecting patient records and other sensitive information from increasingly frequent and sophisticated cyber threats. To address this challenge, the organization decided to deploy a deception strategy that involved creating fake patient records and simulated health information systems. The goal was to detect unauthorized access attempts and gather intelligence on attackers' methods and objectives.

The deployment of this deception technology involved several key challenges. Ensuring that the fake patient records and health information systems were both realistic and secure required close collaboration between the organization's IT and security teams. The deceptive elements had to be designed in such a way that they would attract attackers without compromising the integrity of the actual patient records. Additionally, integrating the deception technology with the organization's existing security infrastructure required careful planning to ensure that alerts from the fake systems were accurately detected and prioritized.

The results of the deception strategy were highly positive. The fake patient records and simulated health information systems successfully attracted several attack attempts, providing the organization with critical insights into the methods used by cybercriminals targeting sensitive healthcare data. The information gathered from these interactions helped the organization enhance its security posture by identifying and addressing vulnerabilities that could be exploited by attackers. Furthermore, the implementation of deception technology contributed to a reduction in false positives and improved the organization's overall threat detection and response capabilities.

In the telecommunications industry, a major service provider faced significant security challenges related to protecting its network infrastructure and customer data. The company chose to implement a deception strategy focused on deploying fake network nodes and simulated customer interactions designed to lure and engage potential attackers. The objective was to improve the detection of network intrusions and gather actionable intelligence on adversaries' tactics and techniques.

The deployment of this deception technology presented several challenges, including the need to ensure that the fake network nodes were indistinguishable from genuine infrastructure components. The company's security team had to design and deploy the decoys in such a way that they would attract attackers without disrupting legitimate network operations. Additionally, integrating the deception technology with the company's existing network monitoring and incident response systems required careful coordination to ensure that alerts from the deceptive elements were properly managed and analyzed.

The results of the deception strategy were highly effective. The fake network nodes and simulated customer interactions successfully attracted several targeted attacks, providing the company with valuable insights into the methods and objectives of cybercriminals targeting its network. The analysis of these interactions allowed the company to enhance its defensive measures and improve its overall security posture. The implementation of deception technology also contributed to a reduction in response times and an improvement in the company's ability to detect and address potential security incidents.

These case studies illustrate the diverse applications and effectiveness of deception technology across various industries. The challenges faced during implementation ranged from ensuring the realism of deceptive elements to integrating them with existing security systems. However, the successful outcomes of these strategies demonstrate the value of deception in enhancing threat detection and improving overall security posture. By learning from these real-world examples, organizations can gain valuable insights into the practical application of deception technology and apply these lessons to strengthen their own security practices.

CHAPTER 26:

In exploring the evolving landscape of cybersecurity deception, it is evident that advancements in technology will play a pivotal role in shaping its future. One prominent development is the enhancement of machine learning (ML) and artificial intelligence (AI) capabilities, which are set to transform the nature and effectiveness of deception strategies. These technologies enable the creation of increasingly sophisticated and dynamic deceptive environments, capable of mimicking genuine systems with greater accuracy.

AI-driven deception systems are poised to offer a more responsive approach to cybersecurity threats. By leveraging AI algorithms, these systems can analyze and interpret large volumes of data to detect and respond to unusual patterns indicative of malicious activity. The integration of AI allows for the real-time adjustment of deceptive tactics based on the behavior of potential attackers. For instance, if an attacker employs a new tactic or exhibits an unusual pattern, AI systems can modify the deceptive elements—such as altering the configuration of decoys or introducing new fake assets—to better align with the threat and enhance the likelihood of detection.

Moreover, the use of AI in deception is not limited to defensive measures. It also opens up new avenues for offensive deception strategies. By utilizing generative adversarial networks (GANs) and other advanced AI techniques, cybersecurity professionals can create highly realistic and convincing decoys that are difficult for attackers to distinguish from legitimate assets.

This level of sophistication can significantly increase the effectiveness of deceptive strategies, making it more challenging for adversaries to discern between genuine and deceptive elements within a network.

Another important development is the expansion of deception into cloud environments and hybrid IT infrastructures. As organizations increasingly migrate to cloud-based solutions and adopt hybrid models that blend on-premises and cloud resources, the scope of deception must evolve to address these new complexities. Future deception strategies will need to incorporate cloud-native technologies and design principles to effectively protect cloud environments. This includes creating deceptive elements that integrate seamlessly with cloud platforms, such as simulated cloud services or fake virtual machines, which can attract and engage attackers attempting to exploit vulnerabilities in cloud configurations.

In addition to cloud environments, the rise of the Internet of Things (IoT) presents a unique challenge for cybersecurity deception. IoT devices, with their diverse and often limited security features, are increasingly targeted by cyber adversaries. Deception strategies must adapt to encompass these devices, creating realistic and convincing fake IoT environments that can detect and mislead attackers targeting connected devices. This requires the development of new techniques for simulating IoT device behaviors and interactions, ensuring that deceptive elements appear as authentic as possible to engage and deceive attackers effectively.

The evolving threat landscape also necessitates the development of more advanced deception techniques. As cyber threats become more sophisticated, including advanced persistent threats (APTs) and state-sponsored attacks, deception strategies must keep pace with these advancements. Future methods may involve the use of deepfake technology and other cutting-edge techniques to create highly convincing simulations or decoys that challenge even the most skilled attackers. The ongoing research and innovation in these areas will be crucial for maintaining the effectiveness of deception strategies in the face of increasingly advanced adversaries.

Furthermore, the future of cybersecurity deception will be influenced by regulatory and ethical considerations. As the use of deceptive practices becomes more widespread, organizations must navigate the legal and ethical implications associated with their deployment. This includes ensuring that deception strategies comply with relevant regulations and ethical standards, such as data privacy and protection laws. Organizations will need to develop clear policies and guidelines governing the use of deception, balancing the need for effective security measures with considerations for privacy and compliance.

The integration of deception with other security measures is another key trend shaping its future. To enhance the overall security posture, deception strategies must be integrated with threat intelligence, behavioral analytics, and incident response capabilities. This holistic approach ensures that deception is not an isolated tactic but a complementary element within a broader security framework. By aligning deception with other security measures, organizations can improve their ability to detect and respond to threats more effectively, creating a more resilient and adaptive defense system.

Finally, the future of cybersecurity deception will benefit from increased collaboration and information sharing within the cybersecurity community. As threats evolve and become more complex, organizations will gain value from sharing insights and experiences related to deception techniques. This collaborative approach can lead to the development of more effective and innovative deception strategies, as well as the establishment of best practices and standards for their deployment.

In summary, the future of cybersecurity deception is characterized by technological advancements, the adaptation to new threat environments, and the need for regulatory and ethical considerations. By embracing these trends and preparing for the evolving landscape, organizations can enhance their deception strategies and strengthen their overall security posture. As the field of cybersecurity deception continues to evolve, staying informed and proactive will be essential for effectively countering emerging threats and maintaining a robust defense against cyber adversaries.

As we delve deeper into the future of cybersecurity deception, one significant aspect that stands out is the integration of deception with other emerging technologies such as blockchain and quantum computing. Blockchain technology, known for its decentralized and immutable ledger system, holds potential for revolutionizing cybersecurity deception by enhancing the authenticity and integrity of deceptive elements. In this context, blockchain could be used to record and verify the deployment and interactions of deceptive assets, providing a transparent and tamper-proof mechanism to ensure their reliability. This could address challenges related to the maintenance and credibility of deceptive tactics, ensuring that they remain effective and resistant to manipulation by adversaries.

Quantum computing introduces a new paradigm in computational power, which could both pose threats and offer opportunities in the realm of cybersecurity deception. The immense processing capabilities of quantum computers could potentially break existing cryptographic algorithms, making traditional deception techniques vulnerable. However, this same power could also be harnessed to develop advanced deception methods. For instance, quantum-based encryption techniques could enhance the security of deceptive environments, while quantum algorithms could be used to simulate highly sophisticated decoy systems that challenge even the most advanced threat actors. Preparing for and adapting to these advancements will be crucial for maintaining the efficacy of deception strategies.

Another forward-looking trend involves the increased use of automated and autonomous systems in cybersecurity. Automation is set to play a pivotal role in scaling deception efforts and responding to threats in real time. By leveraging automation, organizations can deploy and manage large-scale deception environments with greater efficiency, allowing for the rapid creation and adaptation of deceptive elements. Autonomous systems, driven by AI and machine learning, could further enhance the adaptability of deception strategies, dynamically adjusting decoy behaviors and responses based on real-time threat intelligence and attack patterns.

The integration of deception with advanced analytics and visualization tools is also poised to transform the field. Enhanced analytics capabilities will enable organizations to gain deeper insights into attacker behaviors and interactions within deceptive environments. By analyzing data generated from deceptive tactics, organizations can identify emerging attack vectors and refine their deception strategies accordingly. Visualization tools will play a crucial role in presenting complex data in an accessible and actionable format, helping security teams understand the effectiveness of their deception measures and make informed decisions about their security posture.

Furthermore, the evolving landscape of cybersecurity threats underscores the need for deception strategies to be more adaptable and proactive. As attackers become more sophisticated, their tactics are likely to include evasion techniques designed to bypass traditional detection methods. Future deception strategies will need to incorporate adaptive and proactive measures to stay ahead of these evolving threats. This may involve the use of predictive analytics to anticipate and counter potential attack vectors before they materialize, as well as the development of deceptive tactics that can dynamically evolve in response to changes in attacker behavior.

The importance of interdisciplinary collaboration is another emerging trend in the future of cybersecurity deception. As the field of cybersecurity continues to intersect with various domains such as psychology, behavioral science, and social engineering, incorporating insights from these disciplines will enhance the effectiveness of deception strategies. Understanding the psychological and behavioral aspects of attackers can inform the design of more convincing and targeted deceptive tactics. Collaboration with experts in these fields can lead to the development of innovative approaches that leverage a deeper understanding of human behavior and decision-making processes.

The ongoing evolution of regulations and compliance requirements will also influence the future of cybersecurity deception. As organizations navigate a landscape of increasingly stringent data protection and privacy regulations, they must ensure that their deception strategies align with legal and ethical standards. This includes addressing concerns related to data privacy, transparency, and the potential impact of deception on individuals and organizations. Developing frameworks and best practices that balance effective deception with regulatory compliance will be essential for the responsible and successful deployment of deceptive tactics.

In summary, the future of cybersecurity deception will be shaped by advancements in technology, evolving threat landscapes, and the integration of interdisciplinary insights. Embracing emerging technologies such as blockchain and quantum computing, leveraging automation and advanced analytics, and adapting to the changing nature of threats will be critical for maintaining the effectiveness of deception strategies. Additionally, ensuring alignment with regulatory requirements and fostering interdisciplinary collaboration will contribute to the development of innovative and responsible deception practices. By staying informed and proactive, organizations can navigate the evolving landscape of cybersecurity deception and enhance their ability to protect against emerging threats.

CHAPTER 27:

Integrating deception into governance, risk management, and compliance (GRC) frameworks necessitates a thorough understanding of how these practices interrelate and how deception can be effectively employed to reinforce them. Deception's role in GRC extends beyond merely adding another layer of security; it involves strategically embedding deceptive practices into existing processes to enhance their efficacy and relevance.

When implementing deception as part of a governance strategy, organizations must ensure that deceptive methods are not only technically sound but also aligned with overall governance objectives. Governance encompasses the establishment of policies, procedures, and controls designed to guide an organization's operations and decision-making processes. Deception can bolster governance by providing an additional mechanism to enforce and validate the effectiveness of these controls. For instance, by simulating insider threats or external attacks through deceptive means, organizations can test the resilience of their governance frameworks in real-world scenarios. This proactive approach allows for the identification of potential weaknesses in policy enforcement and helps in refining governance practices to ensure they are robust and effective.

In terms of risk management, deception offers a unique advantage by providing actionable intelligence about threat actors and attack methodologies. Traditional risk management often relies on historical data and theoretical models, which can sometimes overlook emerging threats or novel attack vectors. Deception provides a dynamic and real-time method of risk assessment by actively engaging with threat actors in a controlled environment. This interaction yields valuable insights into how risks might manifest and evolve, allowing organizations to update their risk management strategies accordingly. For example, deploying decoy systems that mimic critical infrastructure can reveal how attackers exploit vulnerabilities and adjust their tactics. The intelligence gained from these interactions informs risk assessments and enables organizations to prioritize their mitigation efforts based on actual threat data rather than hypothetical scenarios.

Compliance with regulatory requirements is another critical area where deception can make a significant impact. Regulatory frameworks often mandate that organizations implement effective security controls and demonstrate their compliance through regular assessments and audits. Deception can enhance compliance efforts by providing tangible evidence of a proactive and comprehensive security strategy. For instance, compliance audits frequently assess an organization's ability to detect and respond to security incidents. By incorporating deception technologies into their security practices, organizations can generate documentation and evidence of their ability to identify and manage threats effectively. This documentation can be used to demonstrate compliance with regulatory requirements and to provide assurance to auditors and regulators that security controls are functioning as intended.

Ensuring that deception aligns with organizational policies and standards involves several key considerations. First, organizations must develop a clear policy framework for the deployment and management of deceptive practices. This framework should outline the scope of deception activities, define roles and responsibilities, and establish procedures for monitoring and reporting. Additionally, the ethical implications of deception must be carefully considered. Deception practices should be designed and implemented in a way that respects privacy and minimizes potential harm. For instance, while deceptive methods can be highly effective, they must be balanced with transparency and fairness to avoid potential conflicts with privacy regulations and employee rights.

The integration of deception into existing GRC frameworks also requires ongoing evaluation and adjustment. As organizational needs, threat landscapes, and regulatory requirements evolve, the use of deception must be continually assessed and refined. Regular reviews of deception practices, coupled with feedback from security, risk management, and compliance teams, help ensure that deceptive techniques remain relevant and effective. This iterative approach allows organizations to adapt to new challenges and opportunities, maintaining alignment with governance, risk management, and compliance objectives.

Moreover, integrating deception into GRC frameworks necessitates a collaborative approach across various organizational functions. Security teams, risk managers, compliance officers, and other stakeholders must work together to align deception strategies with broader GRC goals. This collaboration involves sharing information, coordinating efforts, and ensuring that deception practices are integrated seamlessly into existing processes. Effective communication and coordination among these functions are crucial for the successful implementation of deception as part of a comprehensive GRC strategy.

The deployment of deception technologies within GRC frameworks also requires a thoughtful approach to resource allocation. Implementing and managing deception techniques can be resource-intensive, involving the deployment of specialized tools, the creation of deceptive environments, and the analysis of generated data. Organizations must carefully balance these resource requirements with other priorities and ensure that the benefits of deception justify the associated costs. This involves conducting cost-benefit analyses and making informed decisions about the allocation of resources to maximize the value of deception in achieving GRC objectives.

In summary, integrating deception into governance, risk management, and compliance frameworks involves aligning deceptive practices with organizational policies and standards, enhancing risk management processes, and supporting compliance efforts. By embedding deception into GRC strategies, organizations can improve their security posture, gain valuable insights into emerging threats, and demonstrate a proactive approach to compliance. A collaborative and iterative approach, coupled with careful consideration of ethical and resource-related factors, ensures that deception is effectively integrated into GRC frameworks and contributes to the achievement of overall security and regulatory objectives.

Incorporating deception into governance, risk management, and compliance (GRC) practices involves understanding and leveraging its role to achieve comprehensive security and regulatory objectives. The successful integration of deception into GRC frameworks requires a nuanced approach, addressing various aspects of organizational operations and aligning with established policies and standards.

When integrating deception into GRC frameworks, one crucial aspect is the alignment with governance structures. Governance, as the overarching system of rules, practices, and processes by which an organization is directed and controlled, sets the stage for how security measures are implemented and monitored. Deception technologies can complement governance by providing additional layers of testing and validation for governance controls. For example, organizations can deploy deceptive systems that simulate various threat scenarios, such as insider threats or external attacks, to evaluate the effectiveness of governance controls in real-world conditions. This practical testing helps in assessing whether policies and procedures are adequately enforced and whether they remain effective against evolving threats. By integrating these deceptive practices into the governance framework, organizations can ensure that their controls are resilient and adaptable.

In the realm of risk management, deception plays a pivotal role in enhancing an organization's ability to identify and manage risks effectively. Traditional risk management approaches often rely on historical data and static risk assessments, which may not fully capture the dynamic nature of modern threats. Deception offers a dynamic and interactive method of risk assessment by creating controlled environments that mimic real-world conditions and actively engage with potential threat actors. Through the deployment of deceptive assets such as honeypots and decoys, organizations can observe how attackers interact with these environments, gaining insights into their tactics, techniques, and procedures. This real-time intelligence allows organizations to refine their risk management strategies, prioritize risk mitigation efforts, and address emerging threats more effectively. The ability to continuously test and adapt to new threat scenarios ensures that risk management practices remain relevant and robust.

Compliance with regulatory requirements is another area where deception can significantly contribute. Regulatory frameworks often mandate the implementation of robust security controls and require organizations to demonstrate compliance through rigorous assessments and audits. Deception can support compliance efforts by providing tangible evidence of proactive security measures. For example, organizations can use deception technologies to generate detailed logs and reports that demonstrate their ability to detect and respond to security incidents. These logs serve as evidence during compliance audits, showcasing that security controls are functioning as intended and that the organization is actively engaged in protecting its assets. Furthermore, integrating deception into compliance practices helps organizations stay ahead of regulatory changes by adapting their deceptive strategies to align with evolving requirements.

Aligning deception with organizational policies and standards is essential for ensuring its effective integration into GRC frameworks. This involves developing a comprehensive policy framework that outlines the scope, objectives, and procedures for deploying and managing deceptive practices. The policy should clearly define roles and responsibilities, establish guidelines for the use of deception technologies, and set criteria for evaluating their effectiveness. Additionally, the ethical implications of deception must be carefully considered to ensure that deceptive practices do not infringe upon privacy rights or lead to unintended consequences. By developing a well-defined policy framework, organizations can ensure that deception is implemented in a manner that is consistent with organizational values and regulatory requirements.

Ongoing evaluation and adjustment of deception practices are also crucial for maintaining alignment with GRC objectives. As organizational needs, threat landscapes, and regulatory requirements evolve, it is important to regularly review and update deception strategies. This iterative approach involves assessing the effectiveness of existing deceptive practices, gathering feedback from security and compliance teams, and making necessary adjustments to address new challenges and opportunities. Regular reviews help ensure that deception remains a relevant and valuable component of the GRC framework, continuously contributing to enhanced security posture and regulatory compliance.

Effective integration of deception into GRC frameworks also requires collaboration across various organizational functions. Security teams, risk managers, compliance officers, and other stakeholders must work together to ensure that deceptive practices are aligned with broader GRC goals. This collaboration involves sharing information, coordinating efforts, and integrating deceptive techniques seamlessly into existing processes. By fostering a collaborative approach, organizations can ensure that deception is effectively utilized to support governance, risk management, and compliance objectives, enhancing overall security and regulatory outcomes.

Resource allocation is another important consideration when integrating deception into GRC frameworks. Deploying and managing deception technologies can be resource-intensive, involving the acquisition of specialized tools, the creation of deceptive environments, and the analysis of generated data. Organizations must carefully balance these resource requirements with other priorities, conducting cost-benefit analyses to ensure that the benefits of deception justify the associated costs. Informed decisions about resource allocation help maximize the value of deception in achieving GRC objectives, ensuring that it contributes effectively to security and compliance efforts.

In summary, integrating deception into governance, risk management, and compliance frameworks involves aligning deceptive practices with organizational policies, enhancing risk management processes, and supporting compliance efforts. By embedding deception into GRC strategies, organizations can improve their security posture, gain valuable insights into emerging threats, and demonstrate a proactive approach to compliance. A collaborative and iterative approach, coupled with careful consideration of ethical and resource-related factors, ensures that deception is effectively integrated into GRC frameworks, contributing to the achievement of comprehensive security and regulatory objectives.

CHAPTER 28:

A critical aspect of managing and maintaining deception systems is ensuring that they are effectively integrated into the organization's overall security infrastructure. This integration involves aligning deception technologies with existing security policies, incident response protocols, and monitoring systems. The objective is to create a cohesive security environment where deception tools work synergistically with other security measures to enhance overall protection.

To achieve this integration, it is essential to ensure that the deception systems are configured to interact seamlessly with other security technologies such as Security Information and Event Management (SIEM) systems, intrusion detection systems (IDS), and threat intelligence platforms. This involves setting up appropriate data feeds and alerts so that any interaction with deception assets is logged and analyzed in conjunction with other security events. By correlating data from deception systems with other sources of security information, organizations can gain a more comprehensive view of their threat landscape and improve their ability to detect and respond to potential threats.

Effective integration also requires that the deception systems are tailored to fit the specific needs and objectives of the organization. This means configuring the deceptive elements to reflect the organization's unique operational environment and threat profile. For instance, if an organization operates in a highly regulated industry, its deception systems should be designed to address the specific compliance requirements and threat vectors relevant to that industry. Customizing the deception environment in this way helps ensure that the tools provide maximum value and relevance in the context of the organization's security strategy.

Maintaining the relevance and effectiveness of deception systems also involves staying abreast of developments in both technology and threat landscapes. Regularly reviewing advancements in cybersecurity technology and emerging threat trends allows organizations to adapt their deception strategies accordingly. This proactive approach includes evaluating new deception techniques and technologies that may offer enhanced capabilities or improved effectiveness. For instance, advancements in machine learning and artificial intelligence could provide new opportunities for creating more sophisticated and dynamic deceptive environments. By continuously exploring and incorporating these advancements, organizations can ensure that their deception systems remain cutting-edge and capable of countering the latest threats.

In addition to technological advancements, staying informed about evolving threat tactics is crucial for maintaining effective deception systems. Threat actors are constantly developing new methods for evading detection and exploiting vulnerabilities. To counteract these tactics, deception systems must be updated to mimic the latest attack methods and vulnerabilities. This requires a continuous process of threat intelligence gathering and analysis to identify emerging trends and adapt the deception environment accordingly. Regular threat assessments and intelligence sharing with industry peers can provide valuable insights into the latest attack vectors and techniques, helping to inform the ongoing evolution of the deception strategy.

Another important aspect of managing deception systems is ensuring that they are adequately supported by organizational resources. This includes not only financial resources for purchasing and maintaining the necessary technologies but also personnel resources for managing and operating the deception tools. Effective management requires skilled professionals who are knowledgeable about both the technical aspects of the deception systems and the broader cybersecurity landscape. Investing in ongoing training and professional development for these personnel helps ensure that they remain proficient in using and managing the deception tools, which in turn supports the overall effectiveness of the deception program.

Regular audits and assessments are also vital for maintaining the health and effectiveness of deception systems. Conducting periodic audits helps identify any potential weaknesses or areas for improvement within the deception environment. These audits should focus on evaluating the performance of the deception tools, reviewing the configuration and implementation of deceptive elements, and assessing the overall alignment of the deception strategy with the organization's security objectives. By identifying and addressing any issues or gaps discovered during these audits, organizations can ensure that their deception systems continue to provide valuable protection and insights.

Additionally, it is important to establish and maintain clear communication channels within the organization regarding the use and management of deception systems. Ensuring that all relevant stakeholders are aware of the purpose and capabilities of the deception tools, as well as their role in managing and responding to deceptive interactions, helps to foster a collaborative and informed approach to cybersecurity. This includes providing regular updates and briefings on the performance of the deception systems, sharing insights gained from deceptive interactions, and discussing any changes or improvements to the deception strategy.

Overall, the ongoing management and maintenance of deception systems require a multifaceted approach that encompasses integration with other security measures, staying current with technological and threat developments, and ensuring adequate support and resources. By adhering to these best practices and continuously evaluating and refining the deception strategy, organizations can maintain the effectiveness of their deception systems and enhance their overall cybersecurity posture.

To maintain the operational effectiveness of deception systems, a thorough and ongoing review process is essential. This process should encompass several critical areas, including system performance, effectiveness, and alignment with the organization's evolving security objectives. Each of these areas requires meticulous attention to detail and a proactive approach to ensure that the deception tools continue to deliver value over time.

System performance is a key area of focus when managing deception systems. This involves monitoring the technical functionality of the tools to ensure they are operating as intended. Performance metrics such as system uptime, response times, and accuracy of deceptive interactions should be regularly reviewed. Any deviations from expected performance can indicate underlying issues that need to be addressed promptly. For example, if a deception tool is failing to capture certain types of interactions or if its performance degrades over time, it may be necessary to investigate and rectify the cause, whether it's a technical malfunction, outdated software, or inadequate system resources.

Evaluating the effectiveness of deception systems involves assessing how well they achieve their intended objectives. This includes measuring the success of deception in detecting and mitigating threats, as well as its role in gathering intelligence and enhancing overall security posture. Key performance indicators (KPIs) for effectiveness might include metrics such as the number of detected threats, the accuracy of threat identification, and the impact on threat actor behavior. Regular analysis of these metrics helps determine whether the deception strategy is meeting its goals and whether adjustments are needed. For instance, if the deception tools are not capturing as many threats as anticipated, it may be necessary to refine the deceptive elements or introduce new tactics to enhance their efficacy.

Aligning the deception system with the organization's evolving security objectives is another crucial aspect of ongoing management. As the threat landscape and organizational priorities shift, the deception strategy must be adapted accordingly. This involves revisiting the objectives of the deception program and ensuring that the tools and techniques in use align with the current security needs. For example, if the organization faces new types of threats or regulatory requirements, the deception systems should be updated to address these changes. This may involve incorporating new types of deceptive assets, adjusting the deployment of existing assets, or integrating additional security measures to support the evolving strategy.

Another important consideration in maintaining deception systems is the need for regular updates and patch management. Like any other software or technology, deception tools require updates to address vulnerabilities, improve functionality, and incorporate new features. Establishing a routine for applying patches and updates ensures that the systems remain secure and effective against emerging threats. It is also essential to stay informed about updates from the vendors of the deception tools and to apply these updates in a timely manner. This proactive approach helps prevent potential security gaps and maintains the tools' effectiveness.

User training and awareness play a significant role in the successful management of deception systems. Ensuring that personnel are well-trained in using the deception tools and understanding their purpose is crucial for maintaining the effectiveness of the systems. This includes providing ongoing training and updates to reflect changes in the deception strategy, new features of the tools, and emerging threat tactics. Additionally, fostering a culture of security awareness within the organization helps ensure that all relevant stakeholders are informed and engaged in the deception program. Regular communication and training sessions can help reinforce the importance of the deception tools and how they contribute to the overall security posture.

In managing deception systems, it is also important to conduct periodic reviews and assessments. These reviews should evaluate the overall effectiveness of the deception strategy, the performance of individual tools, and the alignment with security objectives. Regular assessments help identify areas for improvement and ensure that the deception systems continue to provide value. This can include conducting internal audits, engaging external consultants, or participating in industry benchmarking activities. By maintaining a rigorous review process, organizations can ensure that their deception systems remain robust and effective.

In summary, managing and maintaining deception systems requires a comprehensive approach that encompasses performance monitoring, effectiveness evaluation, alignment with security objectives, regular updates, and user training. By adhering to these best practices and continuously refining the deception strategy, organizations can ensure that their deception systems remain effective in the face of evolving threats and contribute to a stronger overall security posture.

CHAPTER 29:

Integrating deception into incident response and digital forensics involves a strategic approach that aligns deceptive practices with traditional methods of incident management. To begin with, the implementation of deception requires a nuanced understanding of how these techniques can complement and enhance conventional security measures. One of the foremost benefits of deception in incident response is its ability to provide early and actionable insights into adversarial activities, thereby improving the speed and accuracy of the response process.

When a security incident is detected, the initial response is critical. Deception tools, such as honeypots and decoy systems, act as early-warning mechanisms by attracting and engaging threat actors who would otherwise evade detection. For instance, a well-placed honeypot, mimicking a vulnerable system or service, can lure attackers and prompt them to reveal their tactics, techniques, and procedures. The interactions within these deceptive environments generate valuable data that can be used to understand the nature of the threat and the methods employed by the adversaries. This data is essential for crafting an informed response and developing strategies to mitigate the risk posed by the identified threats.

Incorporating deception into incident response involves several key considerations. Firstly, the placement and configuration of deceptive elements must be meticulously planned to ensure they are effective without inadvertently interfering with legitimate operations. Deceptive assets should be deployed in a way that they blend seamlessly with the actual network infrastructure, thus reducing the likelihood of detection by the threat actors. This strategic deployment ensures that the deceptive systems are engaged only by malicious actors and not by legitimate users, thereby preserving the integrity of the operational environment.

During an incident, the data collected from deception mechanisms plays a pivotal role in the investigation phase. The logs and records from honeypots and decoys offer a detailed account of the attacker's activities, including the specific techniques used to exploit vulnerabilities and the progression of the attack. This information can be used to reconstruct the attack timeline, identify the methods of intrusion, and assess the impact on the organization. By analyzing this data, incident responders can gain insights into the attacker's objectives and adapt their response strategies accordingly. For example, if a decoy system is compromised, the data collected can reveal the tools and techniques used by the attacker, enabling responders to develop targeted countermeasures and strengthen defenses.

The forensic value of deception systems extends beyond the immediate response to incidents. The evidence gathered from deceptive environments can be critical in legal proceedings and regulatory investigations. To ensure the admissibility of this evidence, it is essential to adhere to established forensic practices, including maintaining a clear chain of custody, ensuring data integrity, and following legal protocols. This involves documenting the collection and handling of evidence, securing the data from tampering, and preserving the original state of the deceptive systems. By adhering to these practices, organizations can ensure that the evidence obtained from deceptive mechanisms is robust and reliable for use in investigations and potential legal actions.

Another crucial aspect of managing deception in incident response is the continuous evaluation and improvement of deception strategies. As the threat landscape evolves, so too must the deceptive techniques and tools used to counter these threats. Regular assessments of the effectiveness of deceptive assets, including their ability to attract and engage threat actors, are essential for maintaining their relevance and effectiveness. This involves reviewing the performance of honeypots and decoys, updating their configurations based on emerging threats, and refining the scenarios they simulate to ensure they continue to provide valuable insights.

Additionally, the integration of deception with incident response and forensics requires collaboration between different teams within an organization. Security operations, threat intelligence, and forensic teams must work together to ensure that deception mechanisms are effectively utilized and that the data they generate is properly analyzed and acted upon. This collaborative approach helps to ensure that the full potential of deception is realized and that incident response efforts are comprehensive and coordinated.

Training and awareness are also critical components in leveraging deception effectively. Security personnel must be well-versed in the use of deception tools and understand how to interpret the data they provide. Regular training sessions and simulations can help to ensure that incident response teams are prepared to utilize deception strategies effectively during real-world incidents. This training should cover the deployment and management of deceptive assets, as well as the analysis of the data they generate, to ensure that personnel are equipped to handle the complexities of integrating deception into their response efforts.

In summary, the integration of deception into incident response and digital forensics offers substantial benefits in enhancing an organization's ability to detect, investigate, and respond to security incidents. By strategically deploying deceptive elements and leveraging the data they provide, organizations can gain valuable insights into adversarial activities, improve the speed and accuracy of their response, and gather critical evidence for forensic analysis. This approach not only strengthens incident management but also contributes to a more robust overall security posture. As the threat landscape continues to evolve, the effective use of deception will play an increasingly important role in safeguarding organizational assets and maintaining a resilient security infrastructure.

The integration of deception into incident response and digital forensics also brings to light significant considerations for long-term effectiveness and strategic value. When deception mechanisms are utilized, it is imperative to continuously monitor and adjust these tools based on their performance and the evolving threat landscape. This ongoing evaluation ensures that the deception remains relevant and effective, preventing adversaries from adapting to or bypassing these techniques. The role of deception, while initially reactive, should be developed into a proactive component of a broader security strategy.

One critical aspect of maintaining effective deception is the dynamic adjustment of deceptive assets. As threat actors refine their methods and develop new attack vectors, the deceptive environments must evolve correspondingly. This involves regular updates to the configurations and scenarios simulated by honeypots and decoys. For example, if an attacker demonstrates a new technique for bypassing traditional security controls, the deception mechanisms must be adapted to simulate this new technique to maintain their effectiveness. This proactive adjustment not only enhances the detection capabilities but also helps in understanding the attacker's evolving tactics and refining defensive measures accordingly.

The analysis of data obtained from deceptive environments requires a sophisticated approach. To extract actionable intelligence from deception mechanisms, the data must be meticulously examined and correlated with other security information. This involves using advanced analytics and threat intelligence to interpret the behaviors and techniques observed within the deceptive systems. The insights gained from this analysis can inform incident response strategies and provide valuable context for understanding the broader attack landscape. For instance, patterns of behavior observed in a honeypot could reveal not just individual attack techniques but also indicate potential strategic shifts in adversarial tactics, which can be crucial for preemptive defense planning.

Moreover, integrating deception into forensic investigations demands rigorous documentation and adherence to legal and regulatory standards. When deception mechanisms generate evidence, it is crucial to handle this evidence in a manner that upholds its integrity and admissibility in court. This requires meticulous documentation of how the deception systems were configured, how data was collected, and how evidence was preserved. Additionally, forensic investigators must be well-versed in the principles of chain of custody to ensure that evidence remains uncontaminated and reliable throughout the investigative process. The ability to demonstrate the validity and reliability of evidence gathered from deception systems can significantly impact the success of legal proceedings and regulatory compliance.

An effective incident response strategy that incorporates deception also emphasizes the importance of communication and collaboration across different security functions. The insights gained from deception mechanisms should be shared with other teams, such as threat intelligence, security operations, and IT departments. This cross-functional collaboration ensures that the information derived from deceptive environments is integrated into a cohesive response strategy. Furthermore, the experiences and findings from deception-based investigations can provide valuable feedback to improve the overall security posture and inform the development of future deceptive tactics.

Training and awareness play a vital role in maximizing the benefits of deception in incident response and forensics. Security professionals must be adept at understanding and utilizing deception tools effectively. This involves ongoing education and training to keep abreast of new developments in deception technologies and techniques. Additionally, regular exercises and simulations can help teams practice responding to incidents involving deception, allowing them to refine their skills and adapt their strategies in a controlled environment.

Another important consideration is the ethical and legal implications of using deception in security operations. Organizations must ensure that their use of deception aligns with legal and regulatory requirements and that it is conducted in an ethical manner. This includes being transparent about the use of deceptive techniques within the organization and ensuring that they are used responsibly to avoid any unintended consequences or legal issues. Establishing clear policies and guidelines for the use of deception can help mitigate these risks and ensure that deceptive practices are employed in a manner that is both effective and compliant with relevant laws and regulations.

Finally, the integration of deception into incident response and digital forensics should be viewed as part of a broader, comprehensive security strategy. While deception provides valuable tools for detecting and analyzing adversarial activities, it should be combined with other security measures to create a robust defense posture. This holistic approach ensures that the organization is well-equipped to handle a wide range of threats and incidents, leveraging deception as one of many tools in a multifaceted security arsenal.

In conclusion, the integration of deception into incident response and digital forensics enhances the organization's ability to detect, investigate, and respond to security incidents.

By continuously refining deception mechanisms, leveraging data for actionable intelligence, adhering to legal standards, and fostering collaboration, organizations can improve their incident management capabilities and strengthen their overall security posture. This comprehensive approach not only addresses immediate threats but also contributes to long-term resilience and adaptability in an ever-evolving threat landscape.

CHAPTER 30:

The integration of cybersecurity deception into modern security frameworks has brought a transformative shift in how organizations address and manage cyber threats. Throughout the extensive exploration of deception strategies, it has become clear that these techniques offer not just supplementary defenses but pivotal enhancements to an organization's overall security posture. As the landscape of cybersecurity continues to evolve, understanding the impact and future directions of deception will be crucial for maintaining a robust defensive strategy.

One of the central insights is the way deception disrupts the adversary's ability to operate undetected and unchallenged. By introducing elements designed to mislead and confuse attackers, organizations can create an environment where malicious activities are less likely to succeed. This not only aids in detecting intrusions early but also in diverting attackers away from critical systems. The strategic deployment of decoys, honeypots, and other deceptive tactics effectively raises the cost and complexity for adversaries, providing defenders with a crucial advantage.

In evaluating the effectiveness of these strategies, it becomes evident that deception excels in areas where traditional security measures may fall short. The proactive nature of deception —anticipating and countering potential threats before they materialize—enables organizations to uncover vulnerabilities and weaknesses in their defenses. This forward-thinking approach allows for a more dynamic and adaptive security posture, where the organization is not merely reacting to threats but actively working to preempt them.

The ability of deception techniques to provide actionable intelligence is another significant advantage. Through the strategic use of deceptive elements, organizations can gather detailed information about attackers' tactics, techniques, and procedures (TTPs). This intelligence is invaluable for refining security measures, improving threat detection systems, and enhancing overall threat intelligence. The insights gained from observing attacker behavior in deceptive environments enable a more precise and informed approach to threat mitigation.

As we look to the future, several emerging trends and advancements are poised to shape the evolution of deception in cybersecurity. One notable area of development is the increasing integration of artificial intelligence (AI) and machine learning (ML) into deception strategies. These technologies offer the potential to automate the creation and management of deceptive environments, making them more adaptive and responsive to evolving threats. AI-driven deception systems can dynamically adjust to new attack patterns, ensuring that deceptive tactics remain effective against sophisticated adversaries.

Moreover, the expansion of deception techniques into new domains and technologies highlights the need for continuous innovation. For example, the proliferation of Internet of Things (IoT) devices presents both opportunities and challenges for deception strategies. As IoT environments become more prevalent, they also become attractive targets for attackers. Implementing deception within these contexts—such as through deceptive IoT devices or simulated IoT networks—can enhance the security of these increasingly critical components of modern infrastructure.

The ethical and legal considerations surrounding the use of

deception also warrant careful attention. As organizations integrate deception into their security practices, it is imperative to navigate the complex landscape of privacy, legality, and ethical implications. Establishing clear policies and guidelines for the deployment of deception techniques helps ensure that these practices are implemented responsibly and transparently. Addressing issues related to data privacy, the potential impact on non-targeted systems, and the communication of deceptive practices within the organization is essential for maintaining trust and compliance.

Looking ahead, the continued success of deception strategies will depend on the ability to balance innovation with practicality. Organizations must remain vigilant in updating and refining their deceptive tactics to stay ahead of evolving threats. This involves investing in research and development, collaborating with industry experts, and staying abreast of advancements in cybersecurity technology. By adopting a proactive and adaptable approach, organizations can ensure that their deception strategies continue to provide significant value and protection.

In conclusion, the exploration of deception in cybersecurity reveals its critical role in enhancing defense mechanisms, improving incident response, and supporting governance and compliance objectives. The ongoing advancements in technology and the evolving threat landscape highlight the need for continuous innovation and adaptation. By embracing these developments and addressing the associated ethical considerations, organizations can harness the full potential of deception to safeguard their digital assets and maintain a strong security posture.

As we move forward, the integration of deception into cybersecurity practices will remain a dynamic and essential component of a comprehensive security strategy. Organizations that effectively leverage deception will be better equipped to navigate the complexities of the cyber threat landscape, ensuring long-term resilience and security. The journey of deception in cybersecurity is far from complete, and its future will be shaped by ongoing research, technological advancements, and a commitment to ethical and responsible implementation.

As we reach the culmination of this exploration into cybersecurity deception, it becomes evident that the integration of deceptive techniques into security strategies has significantly transformed the landscape of digital defense. This final examination not only synthesizes the core insights and developments discussed but also underscores the ongoing evolution of deception practices and their implications for future security initiatives.

One of the primary observations from our discussion is the remarkable versatility of deception as a security tool. Unlike traditional security measures, which often focus on preventing breaches or detecting anomalies, deception strategies engage adversaries in a way that redirects their efforts and exposes their tactics. This diversionary approach not only enhances detection capabilities but also provides a deeper understanding of attacker methodologies. By embedding deceptive elements within networks, organizations can actively engage adversaries in environments designed to mislead and trap them, leading to more effective and informed responses.

The effectiveness of deception strategies has been evidenced by their ability to uncover and mitigate previously unknown vulnerabilities. In many instances, deploying deceptive elements has revealed critical gaps in security that might have otherwise gone unnoticed. For example, decoys and honeypots have successfully attracted attackers and provided valuable intelligence about their behaviors and techniques. This intelligence, in turn, has facilitated more precise and targeted defensive measures, enabling organizations to better protect their most critical assets.

Looking ahead, several emerging trends are poised to further shape the future of deception in cybersecurity. The continued advancement of artificial intelligence and machine learning holds promise for enhancing the sophistication and adaptability of deceptive techniques. AI-driven systems can analyze vast amounts of data to detect patterns and adapt deceptive tactics in real-time, improving their effectiveness against increasingly complex threats. These technologies enable a more dynamic and responsive approach to deception, where systems can autonomously adjust to new attack vectors and strategies.

Additionally, the rise of complex and interconnected digital environments, such as the Internet of Things (IoT), introduces new opportunities and challenges for deception. As IoT devices become ubiquitous, they present both new attack surfaces and new avenues for deceptive practices. Implementing deception within IoT environments can involve creating simulated device networks or deploying deceptive IoT devices that serve as traps for potential attackers. This approach not only protects critical infrastructure but also provides insights into how adversaries interact with and exploit IoT systems.

The ethical and legal dimensions of deploying deception in cybersecurity must also be carefully navigated. As organizations integrate deceptive practices, it is crucial to address potential concerns related to privacy, legality, and transparency. Establishing clear guidelines and policies for the responsible use of deception ensures that these techniques are employed in a manner that respects individual rights and complies with regulatory requirements. Furthermore, transparent communication with stakeholders about the use of deception helps maintain trust and align deceptive practices with organizational values and legal standards.

The continuous innovation and refinement of deception

strategies will be essential for maintaining their relevance and effectiveness. Organizations must invest in ongoing research and development to stay ahead of emerging threats and evolving attack techniques. This commitment to innovation includes not only adopting new technologies but also collaborating with industry experts, sharing insights, and learning from real-world incidents. By fostering a culture of continuous improvement and adaptation, organizations can ensure that their deception practices remain robust and effective.

In summary, the role of deception in cybersecurity represents a dynamic and evolving facet of modern defense strategies. Its ability to disrupt, detect, and gather intelligence on adversaries underscores its value as a critical component of a comprehensive security framework. The future of deception will be shaped by advancements in technology, the expanding digital landscape, and the ongoing need for ethical and responsible implementation. As organizations continue to explore and refine their use of deception, they will enhance their ability to navigate the complexities of the cyber threat landscape and safeguard their digital environments with greater resilience and effectiveness.

www.ingramcontent.com/pod-product-compliance
Lightning Source LLC
Chambersburg PA
CBHW052148220526
45471CB00004B/1571